Science
of Coaching

SWIMMING

One Week
Loan

One
Week
Loan

Library of Congress Cataloging-in-Publication Data

Science of coaching swimming/[edited by] John Leonard.
    p.   cm.—(Science of coaching series)
    Includes bibliographical references and index.
    ISBN 0-88011-450-9
    1. Swimming—Coaching.   I. Leonard, John, 1948-   . II. Series.
    GV837.65.S38   1992
    797.2'1--dc20   91-12705
                                                                                         CIP

ISBN: 0-88011-450-9 (case)
        0-88011-665-X (perfect)

Acquisitions Editors: Brian Holding and Linda Anne Bump, PhD; **Developmental Editors:** Rob King and Lori Garrett; **Assistant Editors:** Elizabeth Bridgett and Valerie Hall; **Copyeditor:** Wendy Nelson; **Proofreaders:** Stefani Day and Elizabeth Bridgett; **Indexer:** William O. Lively; **Typesetter:** Angela K. Snyder; **Text Design:** Keith Blomberg; **Text Layout:** Tara Welsch; **Cover Design:** Keith Blomberg; **Cover Photo:** Wilmer Zehr; **Illustrations:** Dick Flood and Tom Janowski; **Printer:** Braun-Brumfield

Leisure Press books are available at special discounts for bulk purchase. Special editions or book excerpts can also be created to specification. For details, contact the Special Sales Manager at Human Kinetics.

Printed in the United States of America   10 9 8 7 6 5 4 3 2 1

Leisure Press
A Division of Human Kinetics
Web site: http: // www.humankinetics.com

United States: Human Kinetics, P.O. Box 5076, Champaign, IL 61825-5076
1-800-747-4457
e-mail: humank@hkusa.com

Canada: Human Kinetics, Box 24040, Windsor, ON N8Y 4Y9
1-800-465-7301 (in Canada only)
e-mail: humank@hkcanada.com

Europe: Human Kinetics, P.O. Box IW14, Leeds LS16 6TR, United Kingdom
(44) 1132 781708
e-mail: humank@hkeurope.com

Australia: Human Kinetics, 57A Price Avenue, Lower Mitcham, South Australia 5062
(08) 277 1555
e-mail: humank@hkaustralia.com

New Zealand: Human Kinetics, P.O. Box 105-231, Auckland 1
(09) 523 3462
e-mail: humank@hknewz.com

WITHDRAWN

Contents

Preface

Since the late 1950s, scientists and coaches have studied swimming in a systematic fashion. The field has seen a proliferation of texts, films, videos, and scientific journals devoted in whole or part to learning how people can swim faster. Simultaneously, texts covering the coaching of swimming have also multiplied. All have been valuable to the aspiring coach.

Now our key need as coaches is to separate information that is vital from that which is merely interesting and to apply the vital and accepted information to help our swimmers perform better and enjoy swimming more. In creating *Science of Coaching Swimming*, we have kept these coaching needs in mind. Each chapter covers a vital area of coaching and swimming improvement. You will learn effective coaching strategies developed from the latest advances in motor learning, sport psychology, biomechanics, exercise physiology, sports medicine, and nutrition. Each chapter explains why a particular sport science is important, then explains the central concerns of the science and provides direct coaching applications for the information and problems presented.

I have always believed that the art of coaching is making the complex simple for the athlete. Whether you are a beginning coach or an accomplished elite coach, you can benefit from *Science of Coaching Swimming*. Last summer I spent several days at the Goodwill Games with Nort Thornton, the distinguished coach of the Cal-Berkeley Bears. Our conversations were like a mini coaching clinic: We shared ideas on key topics in improving the performance of the Bears as well as on swimmers ranging from Matt Biondi (world record holder in the 100 M free) to virtual newcomers at the college level. When we were done, I came home to review *Science of Coaching Swimming*, and I discovered that we had virtually reviewed this text, chapter for chapter. Nort also, when planning for his team, goes back to the basics first.

Nort Thornton will find this text useful, as will the thousands of young coaches who aspire to one day be a Nort Thornton. Along the way to their aspirations, they will help young swimmers swim more effectively, and enjoy it more.

In conclusion, I must say that as well as being insightful experts in their fields, the chapter authors for this book have been excellent to work with. I hope you will enjoy using the book as much as I have enjoyed editing it.

John Leonard
Director, American Swimming Coaches' Association

CHAPTER 1

Motor Learning: How to Teach Skills

William S. Husak
Douglas E. Young
California State University, Long Beach

Two young girls, identical twins, were enrolled in a learn-to-swim program that consisted of 10 lessons. The girls were assigned to two different instructors. One instructor was a graduate of a physical education program, was trained in instruction, and had been a high school coach for a number of years. The other instructor was a swimmer on a local college team and instructed only in this summer job.

Although the lesson plans and objectives for these 10 classes were identical, these plans were implemented quite differently by the two instructors. At the end of the program the girl who was assigned to the well-trained instructor was swimming quite well and enjoyed coming to the pool. The second twin, however, had not progressed nearly as well, and the mother reported that the girl did not enjoy the lessons or swimming.

WHY MOTOR LEARNING IS IMPORTANT

Every swimmer first has to learn proper stroke mechanics. How quickly and effectively this learning process occurs is directly related to the teacher's skills. After acquiring the proper mechanics, a swimmer continues to fine-tune the strokes. Expert coaching will develop the potential in each athlete.

Swim coaches must constantly teach, evaluate, and maximize performance. An effective and wise coach evaluates and teaches both traditional and new concepts and techniques to swimmers, knows how to correct poor technique, and plans in-season and off-season practice. You will be able to do this most successfully if you are well versed in the principles involved in learning and performing swimming skills—particularly the principles that enable your swimmers to acquire the movement components necessary to properly execute swim strokes. It is also important to schedule and structure your practices to maximize this learning and to ensure that your swimmers are at their highest levels of performance at the right time in the season. This chapter presents information and guidelines from the developing field of motor learning that will help you achieve these two goals.

Today's swimming coach must be aware of the information available from the fields of biomechanics, exercise physiology, psychology, nutrition, and sports medicine. But this information can help your swimmers only if you have developed the necessary coaching knowledge and skills to present and apply this information. You need to know about individual differences, the use of feedback, motivation, and constructing practice schedules that maximize learning, transfer, and performance. You must also design your practices so that this knowledge can be imparted to and assimilated by your athletes. Once again, motor learning can aid you in achieving these goals.

MOTOR LEARNING CONCERNS IN SWIMMING

The various areas of study in the field of motor learning have a great deal to offer the swim coach. The following sections sketch these areas and provide practical examples of their application. The first section addresses the individual differences that are found within all populations of athletes, including swimmers. This is followed by a discussion about the use of feedback and how it may be applied to learning situations. Motivation is also discussed as an important factor in learning and performing motor skills—the motivation section presents methods you can use to increase your athletes' motivation, whether for a season or for an upcoming meet. The next section describes how to structure practices to enhance learning and transfer. Each of these factors has a great influence on swimming performance. The final section tells how to put these principles (see Figure 1.1) into practice for the benefit of your swimmers. If you incorporate this knowledge with the information presented in the other chapters, you will be prepared to meet the challenges of coaching your swimmers and helping them fulfill their potential.

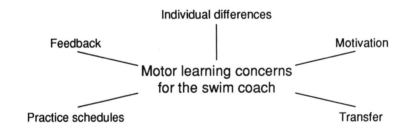

Figure 1.1   Motor learning variables that the coach should consider.

Individual Differences

When coaches look at their teams, they often see the forest and not the trees, forgetting that the team is made up of many individuals, each bringing her or his own particular attributes. Swimmers are individuals, with different abilities and potentials, so you must expect a wide range of performance and learning during your swimmers' seasons and careers.

What factors contribute to these differences, and how might they affect swimming performance? The following sections answer this question and discuss the variables that influence individual differences.

Genetics and Environment

Researchers in the field of genetics have been able to show that at the point of conception we are endowed with a genetic blueprint that sets the boundaries for many of the traits we possess. Some of the more obvious traits are the easily observable physical characteristics such as height, weight, gender, and body shape (somatotype).

In addition to these obvious physical traits, motor behavior researchers have identified certain abilities that influence movement performance. These include reaction time, psychomotor coordination, and arm movement speed. Each of these physical and motor traits may play an important role in determining the ultimate level of performance a swimmer can achieve.

Within these genetic boundaries, some individuals will develop these traits more than others. How are these traits developed? Very often this is a function of the environment the individual grows up in. For example, body growth may be influenced by diet during the formative years, and the development of motor abilities depends on the types of activities the child participates in during this same time period.

By the time a potential swimmer reaches high school, most of these abilities have been established. Swimmers will, therefore, have unique sets of abilities simply based upon their genetic makeups and the environments in which they have spent the first 14 to 18 years of their lives.

Population Differences

In addition to genetic and environmental differences, there are also population differences. For instance, at the high school level a swim team consists of both male and female swimmers at various stages of puberty. Some will not yet have begun puberty, and others will have totally completed puberty. The physical and emotional changes that coincide with the biological changes will affect the performance and attitudes of swimmers in practice and competition. There are many other population differences that may influence individual differences, including socio-economic status and personality. Any of these factors can influence a swimmer's motivation and desire to excel.

It is important to realize that even though you are working with a team, that team is composed of individuals. Each individual brings a special set of abilities and goals. The successful coach can assess performance from both an individual and a group perspective and determine, from that information, how to provide feedback, maintain motivation, and design practice so that the performance and learning of the individual swimmer and team will improve.

Feedback

In all activities, including swimming, feedback is essential for learning and effective performance. Because of the powerful role feedback has on learning and performance, strive to make good use of it and reap the advantages it offers.

What is Feedback?

Each of your swimmers receives an enormous amount of movement-related information during and immediately after a swimming activity. This information is termed "feedback" because information is sent back into the swimmer's central nervous system. Feedback can be classified as either intrinsic or extrinsic. *Intrinsic feedback* refers to internal sensory organs (such as visual, auditory, tactile, and proprioceptive sensory receptors) that provide the swimmer with task-related information about the movement, the environment, and goal achievement. In contrast, *extrinsic feedback* is information received by the swimmer from an external source, such as a coach (Table 1.1). This situation-specific extrinsic feedback is what you should utilize to enhance performance and learning.

Table 1.1
Different Forms of Information Feedback

Types of feedback	
Intrinsic	Extrinsic
Visual	Knowledge of performance (KP)
Tactile	Knowledge of results (KR)
Auditory	Social reinforcement (SR)
Proprioceptive	

Content of Feedback

The informational content of feedback can vary depending on its purpose or intent and should be specific to each situation. For example, if you are correcting a flaw in a swimmer's stroke, your feedback should refer to particular aspects of the pattern of action (such as elbow position). This type of information is referred to as knowledge of performance (KP). Feedback could also inform a swimmer about the movement with respect to the success achieved in competition. This is referred to as knowledge of results (KR); an example of KR is the time elapsed from the "bang" of the starting gun until the initiation of the dive off the starting block. Finally, you can use feedback to reinforce desired behavior. This type of feedback is often referred to as social reinforcement (SR).

Not surprisingly, coaches provide these different types of feedback for specific reasons and in certain situations. However, just providing feedback does not guarantee a temporary or permanent change in your swimmers' performance. To better understand how behavioral changes can be established, let's look at how feedback functions in practice and learning.

Functions of Feedback

Extrinsic feedback, regardless of the informational content, has been shown to function in a variety of ways. First, and perhaps most importantly, it provides information about behavior that is essential for learning; without feedback, performers generally fail to learn a skill and almost never reach high levels of proficiency. Second, feedback provides guidance to performers by directing responses toward the optimal or desirable outcome. Third, feedback can give performers positive and negative reinforcement for their behavior. Finally, feedback can motivate performers to work harder and longer, both of which are desirable in the learning process.

As coach, you are the major provider of feedback for your swimmers. Your feedback can determine both their rate of learning and their ultimate performance. By learning the basic principles and timing of feedback, you can make use of feedback's four functions to optimize its positive effects on your swimmers.

Providing Feedback

The point at which feedback is provided during practice is of critical importance. Allow your swimmers enough time after they have completed some movement or activity to evaluate their own intrinsic feedback, and provide sufficient time for the extrinsic feedback (the information you provide) to be processed (Figure 1.2). To accomplish this, feedback generally should be provided after the completion of a swim and not during the activity. This allows performers to evaluate what they felt, through intrinsic sensory mechanisms, and determine how to correct deficiencies based on your extrinsic feedback. As a general rule, more precise information takes longer to process. In addition, children require more time to process this information effectively than adults, and the less skilled require more time than experts.

Another important guideline is that you should not provide too much feedback. To the surprise of many coaches, feedback is not constantly necessary. Initially, swimmers may need a lot of information to develop proper techniques and patterns of action. However, as they acquire the

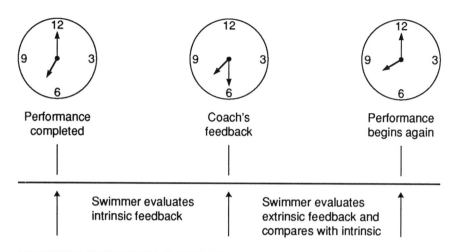

Figure 1.2   A representation of what is occurring before and after feedback is presented.

skill, you should decrease the amount of feedback you provide. In this way, you can direct your swimmers toward the correct behavior without their becoming dependent on feedback for effective performance. One beneficial feedback schedule would provide information very frequently early in the learning process but systematically reduce this amount after the basic fundamentals have been acquired.

What you say as feedback is also very important. Always use terms your swimmer understands; otherwise your feedback will have no effect on the swimmer's performance. And always try to match the content of your feedback to the level of the swimmer's understanding of the skill. The precision of information should vary according to the same types of rules. Don't be vague. Feedback that is not specific (e.g., telling a swimmer that her or his performance was "wrong") rarely is useful. Instead, a statement that quantifies the nature of the problem (e.g., "Your legs were moving too slowly—move your legs faster") is more effective.

Information feedback can be one of your most powerful tools as a coach. By providing the appropriate type of information at the proper time, you can accelerate your swimmers' rate of learning and enhance their ultimate level of performance. Swimmers don't acquire proper swimming skills if they don't get feedback regarding outcome and movement. And these types of feedback can maximize performance, especially when used in conjunction with social reinforcers. Unfortunately, there is no single schedule of feedback that is most effective for all swimmers. Remember, though, that your swimmers need time to process feedback and that intermittent schedules of feedback during practice appear to be most effective for meet situations.

Motivation and Motor Learning

As a coach, you have been aware of swimmers who perform well at one point in the season but perform poorly at others; swimmers who swim well in practice but not in a meet; swimmers who are enthusiastic one year but lose that enthusiasm the next. In each of these situations, the athletes' motivation could explain the behavior. Would it not be wonderful if you could control motivation so each of your swimmers could become the best that she or he could be?

Motivational Levels and Performance

The problem of motivation has received a great deal of attention, and this area of study is tremendously large and complex. Hundreds of textbooks and articles have been written on the topic. For our purposes, we will define motivation as the force behind initiating, maintaining, and determining the intensity of a swimming behavior. From this perspective, it is important for you to know the factors that (a) determine why an athlete wishes to become a swimmer, (b) will keep the athlete a swimmer and prevent him or her from dropping out of a program, and (c) can maximize a swimmer's performance in competition. To accomplish this, you need to understand the relationship between motivation and performance. Each swimmer is unique, and one swimmer may perform well under high levels of motivation whereas another may not.

Nearly everything discussed in this chapter interacts with a swimmer's motivation. Certainly, individual differences, the manner and type of feedback provided, and how practice is structured are factors that affect motivation. Perhaps the simplest rule to understand in coaching is that there is a positive relationship between learning and motivation. That is, as a swimmer improves, motivation tends to increase or remain high. If a swimmer fails to see improvement, motivation tends to decrease. When motivation is low, the swimmer will perform at less than the desired level (Figure 1.3).

A swimmer will evaluate her or his improvement over the course of a season through performance results. Performance is a better reflection of learning in high school swimming than in college swimming because of the differences in training and competition schedules. Very often the high school swimmer trains by swimming approximately 4,000 yards in a typical day of practice. Also, high school swimmers primarily compete in weekly dual meets, so they must be well rested for their performance to be at its peak. College or club swimming is quite different. It is not unusual for these swimmers to train twice a day and swim as much as 20,000 yards during those two workouts. The many hours they spend training tends to leave them tired. As a result, their performance tends to decrease over the course of the season simply because of fatigue. The coach will

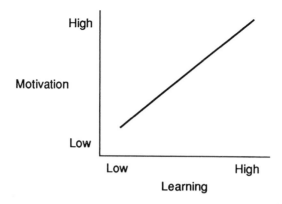

Figure 1.3   The relationship between motivation and learning.

often observe a decrease in motivation during this time of hard training because performance does not improve. It is also not unusual to observe an increase in motivation during the tapering portion of the season when performances begin to improve again.

Short- and Long-Term Motivation

Over the course of a year, you will be concerned with both short- and long-term motivation. The short-term motivation may include preparing for that day's practice or meet. Long-term motivation will involve maintaining motivation over the course of the season or working out in the off-season. All of the factors that will be discussed next may be applied in both the short and the long term, occasionally with certain modifications.

Activation and Motor Learning

A well-established relationship states that there is an optimum level of activation for each individual that will lead to maximum performance (see chapter 2 for specifics). Being above or below that level will result in less than ideal performance. This activation level includes not only the athlete's physical activation (flow of adrenalin, central and peripheral nervous system activity, etc.) but also her or his mood or emotional status. Other terms associated with activation are *arousal* and *anxiety*. Each athlete has her or his own unique, optimal level of activation that will permit the best performance.

Factors Affecting Activation

Do athletes reach this optimum level of activation on their own? Is this level of activation similar to a roll of the dice, so that the best you can do is hope that your swimmers will appear on the pool deck optimally activated for a particular practice or meet? In fact, there are techniques you can use to achieve proper levels of activation.

Many factors can be used to manipulate the level of activation and attention in swimmers (see Table 1.2). One factor is variety. It is important to introduce as much variety as possible in the practice. Variety elevates athletes' activation levels. Repetitive practice sessions leave the swimmer bored and disinterested. Variety can be added by, for instance, alternating the emphasis in practice between stroke mechanics and physical training and by employing different drills or strategies in each of these areas. Be sure each practice is different from the preceding one, and keep your swimmers somewhat unsure about what will be occurring next—this will increase their levels of activation.

Table 1.2
Factors You Can Manipulate to Influence Activation Levels

	Activation Factors	
To decrease activation	Factor	To increase activation
Decrease	Variety	Increase
Decrease	Meaningfulness	Increase
Decrease	Sensory input	Increase
Decrease	Exercise	Increase
Decrease	Uncertainty	Increase
Decrease	Importance	Increase

Meaningfulness is another factor that influences activation. Reminding the swimmer of the importance of a particular workout to the overall goal will make that workout more meaningful to the athlete. Informing swimmers why a particular drill or part of practice is important for training (learning and performance) will enhance the relevance of the drill. Therefore, any time that you are able to introduce meaningfulness into the practice, you will be increasing activational levels and directing more attention to the most important items.

Increasing sensory input tends to increase activation. In competition, the noise of the crowd and the competition itself increase activation. For some meets swimmers shave their bodies, ostensibly in an effort to reduce drag in the water, which leads to faster times. But another possibility is that shaving increases the sensitivity of the neural receptors and heightens awareness, which in turn increases the swimmer's activation level. Another factor influencing activation is the change in temperature swimmers experience when they jump into the water. This sometimes-drastic change can severely decrease activation levels. So it is important that your swimmers become accustomed to the water temperature before competition. This can be accomplished by a brief warm-up period in the water just before the event.

Another variable that has been shown to influence activation levels is exercise. Research has indicated that mild workouts on the morning of competition (at least 4 to 6 hours before the meet) will result in a more optimal level of activation during the meet and, therefore, improved performance. It seems that exercise increases activation in performers who are underactivated and decreases activation for those who are overactivated. This may be especially beneficial for some of the less physically exhausting events, such as diving. A diver's workout could consist of the dives to be performed in competition that day.

Two other factors you can control to alter activation levels are the uncertainty and importance of the competition. The general rule is that competitions that are very important and have a high degree of uncertainty about the outcome will result in higher levels of activation, compared to competitions that are less important and have a low degree of uncertainty. To increase activation levels, simply make statements such as "This is the most crucial meet of the season" (importance of the meet) or "This team has just as good a chance of beating us as we do of beating them" (uncertainty of the outcome). Statements such as "This meet is just like another practice" or "We should have no trouble in beating this team" will have the opposite effect, reducing the level of activation.

You can use variety, meaningfulness, awareness of the environment, exercise, and emphasis on the importance and uncertainty of an event to increase or decrease activation levels. Although these are very effective for the short term, they may also be used for the long term. In particular, if at the beginning of the season you identify specific meets your swimmers should train for, or if you emphasize the uncertainty of a particular event, you will insure that your swimmers' motivation will increase as the events come closer in time. (Psychological strategies for optimizing motivation appear in chapter 2.)

Reinforcement and Punishment

One way to elicit desired behavior is to use reinforcement and punishment techniques. Reinforcement may be defined as any event that increases the probability that a behavior will occur again. Reinforcement can be either positive or negative. Positive reinforcement is said to exist when, after a response happens, the reinforcement results in the behavior occurring again. Praising swimmers (positive reinforcement) for good efforts (the desired behavior) after a practice has the effect of maintaining or increasing those efforts in the next practice. Negative reinforcement occurs when you remove the threat of punishment. An example of negative reinforcement may occur after a poor practice. In this situation, suppose you say that the effort in the next practice must improve (the desired behavior) or swimmers won't be allowed to participate in an upcoming meet (threat of punishment). If the swimmers do have a better practice, the swimmers will be allowed to compete (removing the threat of punishment), and the result is that you have successfully used negative reinforcement. In both of these cases of positive and negative reinforcement, you have increased the probability that the desired behavior will occur.

In contrast, punishment has the opposite effect. Punishment may be defined as any event that decreases the probability of an undesired behavior occurring again. To continue with the previous example, if the swimmers come back the next day and do not give the necessary effort (undesired behavior), then increasing the distance (punishment) may be beneficial to eliminating the lack of effort. Only the resulting behavior on the following day of practice will tell the coach if the punishment strategy has worked. Both reinforcement and punishment techniques are effective, but try to use reinforcement rather than punishment as often as possible, because of its long-term beneficial effects.

In teaching or modifying strokes, reinforcement can be very effective. Strive to highlight the improvement or change that has occurred—for instance, provide verbal encouragement, use videotapes to reinforce the correct execution of the skill, and emphasize the effect of the change on performance (such as swim time). Such strategies will alter old, undesirable behaviors to the desirable, new behaviors, have a positive effect on the learning of a swim skill, and promote a good attitude toward the sport.

Goal Setting

Perhaps one of the most ignored areas influencing the learning and performance of swimming skills is the establishing of goals. Goals provide a direction for the effort the swimmer needs to exert to accomplish the desired outcome (see Figure 1.4). Goals should be both team and individual in nature as well as short-term and long-term.

It is wise to start the season by establishing with the team the goals they wish to achieve. In addition, meet with each individual to identify her or his level of expectation for the year. As the season progresses it may be necessary to modify the goals depending on whether they were too easy or too difficult to achieve. Short-term or immediate goals should be estab-

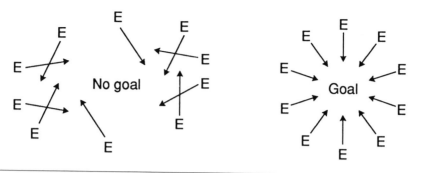

Figure 1.4 Effort that is directed toward a goal is more intense and purposeful.

lished with the long-term goal in mind. For example, identify the purpose of that day's practice and relate that purpose to the times that should be achieved for the upcoming competition (those times should be consistent with the plan for achieving the long-term goals).

Eventually, as the season progresses, the long-term goals established at the beginning of the season become short-term goals. To maintain the highest levels of motivation for the season, long-term goals should have a probability level of under 50% when initially established (Figure 1.5). In other words, long-term goals should be difficult to achieve. Short-term goals, however, should have a much higher probability of success (80% to 100%). The benefit of this type of goal setting is that success in itself is rewarding and reinforcing. Success will keep your swimmers motivated to continue to achieve.

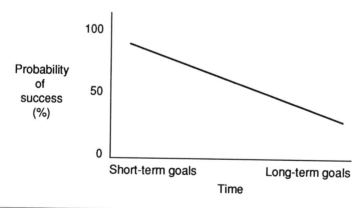

Figure 1.5 A guideline for planning short- and long-term goals, considering the probability of achieving those goals.

Practice

There are many different tools and techniques you can use to teach a skill. Clearly, one of the most important factors is to be sure your practices have the appropriate form. Because practice has such an influential role on learning and performance, be sure you structure your practices carefully. In this section, we will discuss a few procedures you can use to enhance the processes involved in learning.

Practice and Learning

The goal of most practice sessions is to improve performance, but in our view this is not the correct objective for practice. "Shortcuts" that lead to temporary changes are undesirable because the behavioral alterations will be forgotten and not implemented in competition. Instead, the purpose of a practice session should be to enhance learning, or habit strength. This will enable your swimmers to produce appropriate behaviors in a meet, where instructional advice is not always possible, and combine stages of learning so that movement becomes efficient and automatic.

Prepractice Conditions

The first place you can start the learning process is before actual physical practice or between practice sessions. All of your swimmers should know the goal of that day's practice. You can inform them of this in the prepractice session. This instruction is usually given verbally, but if technique practice is involved, you should also have the types of movement patterns demonstrated for your swimmers. In other words, inform the swimmers of the proper stroke and skill technique, and how they are coordinated for maximal performance. Models or demonstrations are effective ways to give your swimmers a visual representation of the correct behavior.

Mental Practice

Another useful instructional tool is imagery, or mental practice. Mental practice is one of the most helpful ways that swimmers can practice without actually swimming—which is particularly useful for swimmers who are recovering from an injury. For a discussion of how mental practice can aid performance, see chapter 2 on imagery in sport psychology.

Practice and Rest Intervals

How much rest time should swimmers get during practices? This question has been a concern of coaches and researchers for decades. You should attempt to maximize the time spent in the pool, but you should also allow sufficient time between sets and drills for effective performance. A sufficient time interval between trials allows swimmers to rest and reduce fatigue. Practice schedules that provide little rest tend to cause fatigue and prevent effective information processing. Providing sufficient recovery time will enhance learning and performance.

Variability of Practice

Another significant factor in learning and performance is the variability in a practice session. As in most movement situations, learning to swim competitively requires that a variety of concepts and skills be acquired, including different strokes and strategies for different race distances. How should you organize your practices for your swimmers to efficiently learn these concepts and skills?

One strategy that is especially effective early in the season is constant practice. Constant practice requires that only one skill be performed for an extended period of time in a practice session. However, later in the season it is more beneficial to have variable practices that require the performance of a variety of skills, such as freestyle, backstroke, and breaststroke.

For variable practice sessions, you can structure the variability systematically or unsystematically. A systematic order requires your swimmers to perform a particular stroke for the initial part of practice, a different stroke during the middle, and then a third stroke at the end of practice. This schedule of variable practice is referred to as blocked practice because performers practice the same stroke for a block of time until the next variation is performed.

An unsystematic order has movement variations scheduled randomly with no particular sequence that the swimmer can determine—your swimmers can't predict what stroke or distance they will have to do next. This random schedule creates a difficult setting for performance, but it appears to result in better learning. Because random practice also increases uncertainty, it will increase activation.

Transfer

Transfer of skills can be used to help learn one skill by practicing some other skill. Specifically, your swimmers can practice nonswimming skills that will help them with swimming. For example, pulling and working out with surgical tubing is one type of transfer practice that can affect the arm stroke in the freestyle. Transfer encompasses a large realm of teaching techniques. This section presents the various types of transfer you can use to enhance learning and methods for implementing transfer in practice.

Types of Transfer

There are four types of transfer that are important for swim instruction. The first type is intratask transfer, or the effect that one variation of a skill has on another variation of the same skill. An example here would be pulling in the water with paddles. This type of transfer is very useful, especially in cases where tempo or coordination of movement parts are important in performance. The second type of transfer is intertask transfer, where a completely different skill interacts with a particular swimming skill, such as weight lifting and the transfer of strength to overall swim performance. The effect that one side of the body (e.g., left arm) has on the other side of the body (e.g., right arm) is a third type of transfer. This bilateral transfer should be considered in swimming because both sides of the body are constantly working together, and interference between limb segments should be minimized. Finally, part-whole transfer involves "breaking down" a task into its parts for individual practice before transferring to the whole task. This technique is commonly used in swimming instruction. For example, a kickboard allows only the legs to generate movement to propel the body across the pool. Each of these types of transfer plays an important role in learning and, when used appropriately, can help maximize performance (see Table 1.3).

Table 1.3
Examples of the Types of Transfer

Type of transfer	Practiced skill	To	Actual skill
Intratask	Swimming with paddles		Strengthening arm stroke in crawl
Intertask	Weight training		Muscular strength for crawl
Bilateral	Completing right arm stroke before starting left arm stroke		Strengthening arm stroke in crawl
Part-whole	Practicing arm stroke and kick separately		Combine arm stroke and kick to perform the crawl

Intra- and Intertask Transfer

Intratask transfer may be used in various ways to improve swimming skills. For instance, consider timing. A goal of competitive swimmers is to minimize overall time (such as the time taken to swim a specific distance).

Minimizing time is unquestionably easier said than done; however, using an intratask transfer technique may improve overall time. With methods similar to interval training in track and field, swimming at different rates can lead to positive transfer—or lower overall times. When the swimmer swims at a variety of speeds, the relative timing between segments of the body becomes more coordinated and the body functions as a unit—for example, the timing between how fast the legs and arms must move becomes more apparent. The result is a smoother or less jerky action that can be performed at almost any rate.

Intertask transfer is an alternative method that can be used to improve swimming skills during the off-season. Although many physical educators and coaches believe that there is always some level of positive or negative transfer between skills, very little transfer exists between most skills. The key factor that determines positive transfer is the similarity between skills. This is not to say that other skills will not influence swimming performance, but this influence will generally be very small. Skills or simulators that are very similar, such as playing water polo, strength training, or pulling with surgical tubing, will have beneficial effects. An activity like jogging will have no or little effect. Therefore, to make intertask transfer work, you must be inventive and create movement patterns that essentially are the same as those encountered in the pool.

Bilateral Transfer

It is well established that the movement of one side of the body will significantly affect movement of the other side of the body. Therefore, as your swimmers perform and learn skills, consider how both sides of the body are required to act. Movements that require the body to perform the exact same motion on both sides are easier to perform than other actions. Skills such as the butterfly and breaststroke, where the arms and legs mirror each other, are much easier to perform than a freestyle stroke and could be among the first skills acquired by beginning swimmers. The freestyle, being much more difficult to learn, would be more appropriate for swimmers beyond the beginning stage.

Part-Whole Transfer

The other common type of transfer technique used in swim instruction is part-whole transfer. Practicing just the arm movements of the freestyle or backstroke with no leg movement is an example of part-whole instruction. The underlying reason for this instructional technique is that it helps swimmers to concentrate on a specific segment of the movement without the interference of the other moving body parts. In turn, rapid gains in the overall skill will follow. In many cases, this part practice is effective for learning. This is especially true when a skill has sequential parts to it (as in the butterfly stroke) or the arm and leg movements are independent (as in the freestyle).

Negative Transfer

However, we caution that part practice is not always useful and could lead to negative transfer, where practice of one aspect of a skill leads to decrements in performance of the overall skill. Negative transfer will occur in tasks that are not defined in sequence; in these instances, the part practice is not as effective. For example, practicing the arm movements in the breaststroke separate from the leg movements for an extended amount of time is probably not altogether beneficial because the end product requires an intricate timing association between them. And practice of the parts with different timing requirements may hinder the coordination of parts when performed as a unit.

PUTTING MOTOR LEARNING TO WORK FOR YOU

The various topics that have been presented in this chapter can help you maximize the performance and instructional process for your swimmers. But what is the best method of implementing these variables?

The PIE Method

One method that appears to be particularly effective we have termed the praise, instruction, and expectation (PIE) method.

Praise

When instructing or coaching swimmers, it is a good idea to begin by praising some aspect of their previous performance. This not only reinforces the good qualities of the performance that you wish to maintain but also makes the swimmer more receptive and attentive to what is about to follow. Each of us becomes more receptive to criticism when we have just been complimented on some aspect of performance.

Instruction

The second phase of this method deals with the actual instruction. During this phase you are providing specific, constructive criticism that should enhance performance in some way. This instruction should be concise and detailed enough that it can be assimilated by the athlete. You may wish to review the section on feedback for types of information to provide and methods of providing it.

Expectation

The last phase deals with establishing an expectation or goal from the modification in behavior. This expectation should define exactly what the result of the correction will be. This expectation further serves as the goal for future performance and the standard for assessing, praising, and instructing future performance.

An Example of PIE

Let's use this PIE method in a hypothetical situation (see Coaches' Clinic 1.1).

COACHES' CLINIC 1.1: EASY AS PIE

As you observe Jill, you notice she has poor longitudinal body alignment in swimming the crawl stroke. Your conversation with her may progress something like this: "Your crawl stroke has improved a great deal in the last few practices [praise]. I have noticed, however, that your head and shoulders are too high in the water and you are kicking too deep. If you decrease the arch in your back, you will become more streamlined [instruction]. This will result in less resistance in the water, less energy will be spent to overcome the resistance, and therefore you should swim faster [expectation]."

You can be much more complete and detailed in each PIE phase. In addition to the verbal instructions, you can demonstrate or model the technique with videotapes or other swimmers on the team. After you provide the information, the most important factor becomes structuring the practice and your responses to Jill's behavior so that her learning is maximized. If Jill has swum the crawl for years with a deep arch in her back, she will not necessarily be able to correct it immediately. Indeed, even after you observe a correction, it is quite possible that Jill will revert back because of all that previous practice. Therefore, monitoring her performance becomes very important.

Some Other Coaching Tips

A good coach is first of all a good teacher. In swimming, as in most sports, that teaching includes developing not only the physical aspects of performance, but also the cognitive and attitudinal factors of being a competitive swimmer. In other words, learning and performance are a function of not only the physical attributes of the swimmer but also of her or his competitiveness and desire to excel.

Siedentop (1983) proposed some additional considerations for teaching physical skills. He states that a basic consideration is to provide a safe environment in which the athlete can train and learn. This includes careful supervision of activities during practice. Siedentop also recommends that communication be efficient. This means that you should plan what you wish to communicate, use language your swimmers can understand, and talk slowly. Also plan and use demonstrations and visual aids to complement your verbal instructions.

Perhaps the biggest impact you have is in the area of providing feedback. Siedentop identifies the many different types of feedback and recommends that, in general, feedback be positive, specific in nature, and directed toward that aspect of performance that is being focused on. A common error with teams is to provide mostly group-directed feedback. Individualized feedback is essential, and you should stay with the athlete for a sufficient period of time to make the feedback effective. This includes analyzing the effect of the feedback so that it accomplishes what you intended.

It is also critical to monitor performance—not only in the long term but also for the short term. Many coaches chart performance. With computers, it is now fairly easy to produce charts that depict performance in graphic form, and using these can help improve your swimmers' performance and learning.

In summary, knowledge of motor learning can provide guidelines and strategies for maximizing your swimmers' learning and performance. If you can implement these guidelines and strategies, you will better develop your swimmers' potential. Your swimmers will have a positive attitude toward the sport and will experience success, and this individual success will translate into a successful team and season.

KEYS TO SUCCESS

- **Evaluate and teach both traditional and new concepts and techniques.**
- **Know how to correct poor technique.**

- Plan in-season and off-season practice.
- Consider each team as a set of individuals with different abilities.
- Feedback is essential for learning and effective performance.
- Extrinsic feedback is a powerful tool for you.
- The content of feedback should vary depending on its purpose or intent.
- The provision of extrinsic feedback determines the rate of learning and ultimate performance.
- The point in time at which feedback is provided is critical.
- Your swimmers should evaluate their movements and performance via intrinsic feedback mechanisms.
- Extrinsic feedback is not constantly necessary.
- Motivation and learning have a positive relationship.
- Many factors may manipulate activation and attention to facilitate learning and performance.
- Reinforcement increases the probability that a behavior will occur again.
- Punishment decreases the probability that a behavior will occur again.
- Strive to use reinforcement whenever possible.
- Goals provide a direction for effort required to achieve an outcome.
- Practice sessions should be used to develop habit strength.
- The learning process can begin before physical practice.
- Sufficient periods of recovery time will enhance learning and performance.
- Variable practice can improve learning.
- Practice of some skills can facilitate the performance of others.
- A good coach is first a good teacher.

REFERENCES AND RESOURCES

Magill, R.A. (1989). *Motor learning: Concepts and applications* (3rd ed.). Dubuque, IA: Brown.

Martens, R., Christina, R.W., Harvey, J.S., & Sharkey, B.J. (1981). *Coaching young athletes*. Champaign, IL: Human Kinetics.

Siedentop, D. (1983). *Developing teaching skills in physical education* (2nd ed.). Boston: Houghton Mifflin.

CHAPTER 2

Sport Psychology: Mental Training

Jodi Yambor
University of Miami

Ali sits behind the blocks, eagerly looking forward to the start of the 100-yard freestyle at the conference championship meet. She thinks, "I can't wait to swim; I've never been so ready in all my life. I've trained well all season, both physically and mentally, and now I know I am going to have the best swim of my life." She gets up and moves around, stretching some, feeling confident and relaxed. She glances over at Beth, the girl behind the block next to her, who is nervously biting her nails, bouncing her leg, and staring at the floor. "Boy, I've been there before," Ali says to herself. "Thank heaven I've learned to relax, visualize, and mentally prepare myself for my race rather than sitting there wondering and worrying how I am going to do." As Ali steps up on the blocks, nothing exists for her except the race. She is totally focused on the sound of the gun and exploding off the blocks.

Meanwhile, Beth is thinking, "I hope I do well today. I really need to remember to make all the adjustments with my stroke that Coach has been working on. I can't miss any turns, and I need to bring it home without dying." While Beth is worrying about not false starting, the gun sounds. Ali is the first one in the water. She begins swimming looking swift, strong, and powerful, riding high in the water. Beth is the last one to enter the pool. She momentarily thinks of her parents, coach, and friends in the stands and doesn't want to disappoint them. So she immediately begins sprinting to catch the others. She forgets to breathe until right before the first turn. As she comes off the wall her muscles tighten, and they feel like rocks. She begins to ride lower in the water and struggles to stay close. Before long she resigns herself to a finish she half expected, one that was not nearly as good as her previous best. Next to her, Ali is elated. She is already out of the water and being congratulated by her coach and friends on her outstanding swim. "I just knew I was going to have a great swim," Ali tells them.

WHY SPORT PSYCHOLOGY IS IMPORTANT

Sport psychology is important because it links the body with the mind. It is an essential aspect of the Olympic spirit, which calls for a sound mind and body. Most coaches are extremely adept at training the body but spend little if any time training the mind—and yet, when poor performances occur, they frequently blame it on psychological factors. ("You didn't use your head." "You were too uptight.")

The science of sport psychology can help you and your swimmers identify ideal performance states. You can teach your swimmers various performance enhancement techniques that will help them control and adjust the various mental factors, such as concentration and arousal, that contribute to their ideal performance states and increase the probability that peak performance will occur.

Mental skills, just like physical skills, need to be practiced on a regular basis. Don't let your swimmers expect to execute performance enhancement skills perfectly the first time they try them. They need to understand and remember that proficiency develops with practice.

For the greatest benefit to be derived from mental skills training, it should begin the first week of practice and continue throughout the season, and it must be utilized daily during the regular workout. On some days, mental training should be allotted special time during the training session and on other days it can be incorporated into the stretching routine or the warm-up period or utilized between sets.

Swimmers and coaches who learn and practice performance enhancement skills increase the chance that they will realize their maximum potential in their sport. These skills, initially learned to improve sport performance, are also readily applicable to academic, social, and career settings and should be considered performance enhancement techniques not only for sport but for life.

SPORT PSYCHOLOGY CONCERNS IN SWIMMING

In swimming, some specific sport psychology concerns center around performance expectations throughout the course of the season and the outside influences that may affect them. By teaching the use of appropriate attentional styles for workouts and competition, you can maximize your swimmers' readiness. Developing a positive attitude in your swimmers can turn even long, solitary training bouts into truly productive workouts. You and your swimmers can learn to communicate better and develop a healthier and more harmonious relationship. Finally, it is extremely important in the sport of swimming to develop and sustain motivation, in order to help your swimmers avoid burnout.

Communication

Communication is the building block for all relationships. Good communication is critical to positive and enduring interaction between people. Verbal communication is an endeavor to induce a state in another person using sound sequences called words. The nature of the state is dependent on the purpose of the communication. Communication may occur for a variety of reasons—to inform, influence, motivate, negotiate, or establish human contact. The communication process involves two main components, speaking and listening. Most people are not very good listeners and need to develop this skill. Listening is not easy; it requires a high degree of concentration and effort.

A number of guidelines can help improve listening skills. First of all, listen with openness. Secondly, do not attempt to evaluate, judge, or interpret the message while it is being delivered. Listen for the main idea rather than specific points. Give the speaker frequent and direct eye contact; show that she or he has your undivided attention. Do not attempt to formulate your response while listening. "Listen" to the nonverbal messages that are being sent, such as the speaker's body language, use of personal space, and tone of voice. Finally, when the speaker is finished, paraphrase the message back to her or him: "What I think I hear you saying is . . . ."

When speaking, it is very important to send messages that are clear and consistent. Do not expect that others can read your mind. People must be told what you think, feel, want, and need, if you expect them to know this information. Your messages should be direct rather than hinting at or implying something (see Figure 2.1).

Miscommunication

Thoughts before conversation	Conversation	Thoughts after conversation
Coach Even though Scott is my best sprinter, I'm going to let Bob swim the 50 free because today is his last home meet, he is a senior, his parents are here, and he has worked hard all year.	Coach "Scott, I'm going to have Bob swim the 50 free today, and I want you to swim the 200 free."	Coach I'm glad he understands, this worked out well for everyone.
Scott I'm really psyched for this meet. I can win the 50 free today.	Scott "That's fine with me, coach."	Scott I can't believe I don't get to swim the 50 free. I wonder if the coach thinks Bob is faster than me. I hate swimming the 200 free.

Figure 2.1   How communication can become miscommunication.

It is important to claim messages as your own by using "I" as opposed to "we" statements. The verbal and nonverbal messages you send should match. Finally, you need to obtain feedback to determine whether your message was received accurately. A good time to practice this is right after you have spoken to an athlete about his or her swim, especially a negative performance. Ask the athlete to tell you what he or she heard you say about the swim.

Communication is a complex, interpersonal process that can easily go astray, especially when messages travel between a number of different people. This may be caused by the listener physically not hearing or choosing not to hear the entire message, by taking parts of the message out of context, or by interpreting or embellishing the message before passing it on to another person. When the original message is altered in any way, it becomes to some degree a rumor (see Coaches' Clinic 2.1).

COACHES' CLINIC 2.1: THE RUMOR MILL

One method of dealing with this potential problem of rumors is to conduct a rumor clinic with the team. Ask for four volunteers, one who stays with the team and three who leave the room. Then ask the team, especially the volunteer in the room, to listen carefully as they are read a story written about them that is interesting and funny. Next, the volunteer who stayed in the room is asked to call in one of the volunteers from outside and repeat the story out loud to her or him. This process continues until the story has been repeated by each of the four volunteers. Finally, the original story is again read to the group so everyone can hear the changes that have taken place. This process should lead to a discussion of rumor development. This exercise will increase the team's awareness of how and why rumors develop and help to decrease the likelihood of their occurrence on the team.

Motivation

In psychological terms, motivation is the force within the individual that moves her or him toward action. Motivation initiates, maintains, or changes behavior. It influences the individual's choice of activities, the length of time she or he will persist, and the level of performance.

Each individual has a variety of motivators for behavior. Some typical motives for participating in the sport of swimming are to develop skills and competencies, to gain success and recognition, to affiliate and make friends, to exercise and be fit, to release energy, to experience challenges, excitement, and fun, and to receive tangible payoffs. Sometimes athletes may not even be aware of their motives.

Motivation has two basic sources. Intrinsic motivation comes from inside the person and is internally controlled. Extrinsic motivation comes from outside the person and is externally controlled. Intrinsic motivation is the motivation to engage in an activity for its own sake. It is an inner striving to be self-determining and competent. Mastery and success are the goals of intrinsically motivated individuals, and when they are achieved they are their own rewards. Intrinsically motivated athletes swim because they love to swim—it gives them enjoyment and satisfaction. It is fun!

Extrinsic motivation comes from other people and through reinforcements. The reinforcements may be tangible, as with trophies or money, or intangible, as with praise or recognition. Generally, athletes need to have both types of motivation to achieve their potential. However, intrinsic motivation is the more powerful and desirable source of motivation.

Always remember that each swimmer is a unique individual. What positively motivates one swimmer may have little or no effect on another. Therefore, you must communicate with your swimmers individually: Actually ask each one "What can I say or do to help motivate you for practice and competition? Am I doing anything presently that decreases your motivation level for practice or competition?" You can also ask athletes what type of comments from you about their performance most improves their motivation levels for practices and competition.

Goal Setting

Goal setting is the most widely used method of motivation and also the most powerful technique known to improve performance. There are several specific guidelines that should be followed to increase the probability of goal attainment. First, goals should be positive and specific. They should be realistic, conceivable, and believable. Goals need to be challenging, because if they are too easily obtained they lack meaning. On the other hand, if the goals are too hard to reach, the individual will generally become discouraged and eventually quit trying to achieve the goal.

Have your swimmers establish their goals at the beginning of the season with your help. They should write them out and put them in a personal place where they will see them daily (e.g., in their lockers or on the mirror in their bedroom). Team goals can also be set by the members and the coach.

Goals are best set in stepping-stone fashion—short-, medium-, and long-range or perhaps dual-meet, conference-meet, and state-meet goal times. The most important aspect of goal setting involves setting up a plan of action to achieve the goal. A swimmer's action plan would probably include attending and working hard at all swimming practices, improving strength and flexibility through weight training and exercise, eating correctly, and getting enough sleep each night. Most athletes who fail to reach their goals do so because they do not develop or adhere to a well-organized, comprehensive action plan.

Another important aspect of goal setting is to examine possible methods of sabotage. What might keep a swimmer from reaching his or her goal? Perhaps skipping workouts or loafing during practice. What could be done to prevent these types of sabotage from occurring? To reduce the chance of missing workouts, perhaps a teammate could pick up the individual on the way to practice, or maybe the individual could share a locker with a teammate and keep the only key. To help counteract loafing, the swimmer should go first in the lane or swim behind a person who is faster and stay close behind.

Goals should be evaluated on a regular basis and adjusted when necessary. For example, a swimmer who is seriously ill and out of the water for 2 weeks prior to the conference championship most likely will not be able to achieve his or her personal goal. Consequently, you should sit down with this swimmer and discuss the situation and make appropriate goal adjustments.

In swimming, approximately 95% of the time is spent practicing and only 5% competing. However, most people set goals only for competition. Consequently, it is extremely important to set goals for practice as well as competition (see Coaches' Clinic 2.2). Finally, there must be total

---

COACHES' CLINIC 2.2: GOAL-SET SWIMMING

One way to use goal setting in practice is to establish a goal-set swim, which is cycled in with the appropriate physiological training approximately every 2 weeks. For example, if Jacqui's best time in the 100-yard freestyle is 55.0 and her end of the year goal is 53.8, her goal-set swim might be 6 × 100 on 8:00 from a pushoff, and her goal would be to average under 1:00 by the end of the season. Goal-set times should be posted, and you need to give feedback.

---

commitment to the goal, and visualization should be used regularly to assist in goal attainment.

Goal setting enhances performance, and it also improves the quality of daily workouts, relieves boredom during practice, helps clarify expectations, and decreases anxiety. Goal setting is additionally beneficial because it increases an individual's intrinsic motivation, personal pride, self-satisfaction, and self-confidence.

Burnout

Psychological burnout can be especially problematic in swimming, because swimming demands such a considerable expenditure of time and effort. Also, the nature of training tends to be repetitive and can cause boredom. Because it is an individual sport, swimmers oftentimes receive less social support than other athletes from their peers. Burnout occurs most frequently with female swimmers, who often retire well before they reach their physical and psychological peak. This is extremely unfortunate in terms of the unfulfilled potential that might have greatly benefited both the individual and potentially the United States Swimming national program. Fortunately, and most importantly, burnout is not inevitable. There are some warning signs to watch for, including personality traits that may predispose individuals to burnout; physical, behavioral, and cognitive symptoms; and situations or circumstances that seem to increase the likelihood of burnout.

Regarding personality, individuals with perfectionistic tendencies, those who are other-oriented, or those who lack assertiveness appear to be the most prone to burnout. The perfectionist is generally an over-achiever who sets extremely high, sometimes unrealistic, standards and has a strong need to be in control so that things will be done right. People who are other-oriented have a strong desire to be liked and admired, are sensitive to criticism, and treat others much better than they treat themselves. Unassertive individuals find it extremely hard to say no, rarely express negative feelings, and, if they do express them, feel very guilty about it.

Athletes in a burnout state show physical signs such as fatigue, tension, irritability, a decrease in energy level, a decline in performance, a marked rise in sleep disturbances, and an increased susceptibility to illness or injury. Behaviorally the individual is depressed and lonely, may have developed a negative attitude toward swimming, and may show resentment toward you, teammates, or parents. The cognitive symptoms are anxiety, boredom, perceived helplessness, perceived low accomplishment, and lack of enjoyment.

Some factors that lead to burnout include the basic nature of the learning curve (Figure 2.2) and lack of positive reinforcement from you or from parents.

The inflexible use of authoritarian coaching methods and abusive behavior by a coach or parent tend to promote burnout. If your or the parents' expectations are higher than the swimmer's, the swimmer has few decision-making opportunities, and if the athlete perceives that she or he is missing out on life, burnout is much more likely. Finally, burnout is most likely to occur if the season is extremely long without breaks and your swimmers have to endure particularly boring practice sessions.

Some suggestions on decreasing the occurrences of burnout are practicing goal setting to help offset the effect of the learning curve and clarifying

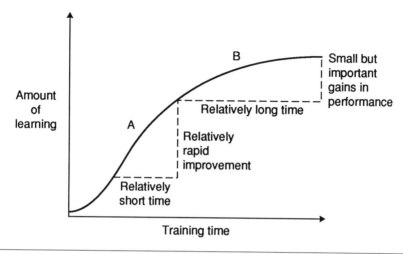

Figure 2.2 Learning time depends upon experience level: Beginning and intermediate athletes (in range A) tend to improve a great deal in a short amount of time; elite athletes (in range B) tend to require a substantial increase in learning time to make even smaller gains.

the athlete's performance expectations for you and the parents. You and the parents need to recognize minor improvement and provide increased positive reinforcement. You must treat all athletes with dignity and respect and allow them some input into their training and into meet and event selection, and time off from their sport.

Make a specific effort to design workouts that have variety and are interesting, perhaps incorporating visualization or group goal setting into the workouts. Don't let your swimmers be too demanding of themselves; encourage them to treat themselves the way they would treat their best friend. Burnout can also be avoided if the athlete seeks out counseling, which can increase self-awareness, help develop assertiveness skills, and assist in overall personal development.

Arousal

Arousal is the level of mental and physical activation an individual is experiencing. It can range from deep sleep to extreme excitement. Generally, individuals perform best under a moderate level of arousal. This is the basic premise of the inverted U theory, which states that as arousal increases, performance improves up to an optimal point, after which, if arousal continues to increase, performance tends to decline (see Figure 2.3).

Remember that each swimmer is different, and that the optimum point of arousal will be different for each one. Therefore, it is important for every swimmer to become aware of her or his optimal arousal level for

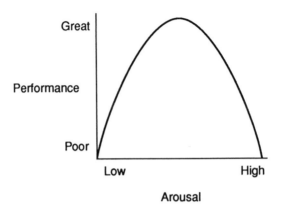

Figure 2.3   The inverted U theory postulates that performance improves up to an optimal level of arousal, then falls off as an athlete becomes overaroused.

peak performance. Next, they need to learn different methods to increase or decrease their arousal level, so that given any situation, they will be able to make the appropriate adjustments to enhance their chances of obtaining a peak performance.

You and your swimmers should be aware that there are a number of somatic (physical) and cognitive (mental) changes that take place when an individual is overaroused (see Table 2.1). Some common behaviors of overaroused individuals are pacing, nail biting, withdrawal, extreme talkativeness, and repetitious behavior.

Although a swimmer's performance may at times suffer from lack of arousal, overarousal is a much more common problem. The most frequently occurring manifestation of overarousal is increased muscle ten-

Table 2.1
Potential Changes Due to Overarousal

Somatic	Cognitive
Increased heart rate	Sense of confusion
Increased breathing rate	Inability to make decisions
Increased muscle tension	Forgetfulness
Sweaty palms	Inability to concentrate
Butterflies in stomach	Resort to old habits
Frequently using the bathroom	Increase in negative thoughts
Cotton mouth	

sion. Some of the negative effects that muscle tension can have on performance are to

- decrease flexibility,
- decrease range of motion,
- decrease coordination,
- increase lactic acid buildup,
- increase the perception of pain,
- increase the frequency of negative thoughts,
- increase muscle soreness and cramping, and
- promote the onset of fatigue by increasing energy expenditure.

Consequently, your swimmers need to learn to reduce their level of arousal by using some type of relaxation technique. The most basic form of relaxation, which everyone has used at one time or another, is deep controlled breathing. Basically the focus is on breathing from the diaphragm rather than the chest. Your swimmers can check to see if they are doing this correctly by placing one hand on the chest and one hand on the abdomen and taking three deep breaths to see which hand moves the most.

Deep controlled breathing can be used effectively by swimmers during practice between sets or even during sets if time allows. It can be used during competition while the swimmer is behind the blocks prior to the start of the race or while waiting his or her turn on a relay.

Probably the most commonly used relaxation technique in sport is progressive muscle relaxation, developed by Dr. Edmund Jacobson. Progressive muscle relaxation is based on the premise that tension and relaxation are mutually exclusive. A corollary of that premise is that an anxious mind cannot exist in a relaxed body. Progressive muscle relaxation involves systematically tightening and then relaxing the major muscle groups throughout the body. Learning to contract the muscles teaches perception of muscle tension; relaxing develops awareness and sensitivity to the absence of tension and the knowledge that it can be voluntarily induced. Besides increasing awareness and control of muscle tension levels, progressive muscle relaxation can

- remove localized tension,
- improve coordination,
- facilitate recovery (after workouts, between events, during a meet, or when traveling),
- improve concentration,
- help reduce prerace anxiety, and
- promote sleep (which is especially important the night before a major competition).

Eventually, the tensing aspect of the technique is left out, and the individual focuses on relaxing the various muscle groups throughout the body.

There are a number of other relaxation techniques, such as autogenics, biofeedback, and meditation, that will not be discussed here. However, visualization, which is the next performance enhancement technique to be covered, can also be used as a relaxation technique.

Imagery

Imagery is the process of creating or recreating a sensory experience without the usual external stimuli. Ideally, it involves the use of all of the senses and emotions. Frequently, athletes only see their performance rather than experience it with all their powers of perception. Usually athletes who use only the visual aspect of imagery do so from an external, or third-person, perspective—as if watching themselves on videotape or stepping outside their bodies and watching themselves perform. The other method of imagery is from an internal, or first-person, perspective. While using internal imagery, your swimmers will see exactly the sorts of things they would see through their own eyes if they were physically performing. They will also experience sounds or smells in their environment, such as the explosion of the starter's gun or your shrill whistle, the scent of chlorine, or the aroma of rubdown lotions. They will also make use of their tactile and kinesthetic senses, such as reaching down and splashing the cool, clear water on themselves or experiencing the feel of their stroke as they move through the water. It is also advisable to include an emotional component, such as the excitement and confidence they feel prior to competing and the thrill and happiness they experience following a successful race.

Before discussing imagery, ask your swimmers if they are already using this skill. If any of them are, find out whether they use an external or internal perspective. Both types can be beneficial, although generally speaking an internal perspective is preferable. An athlete who is already successfully using an external perspective, however, should continue using it.

The more vivid and real your swimmers make the experience, the more potentially beneficial it becomes for them. The mind cannot distinguish between a real event and a vividly imagined event. Consequently, swimmers who visualize every aspect of a race correctly, in advance, will have a greater chance of actually swimming the imagined race, because in a sense they have "swum" the race prior to its actual start.

It is extremely important that your swimmers control their imagery and that their imagery be very specific and positive. Oftentimes athletes visualize things they want to avoid, such as missing a turn. Research has demonstrated that negative imagery produces negative performance. Consequently, it is critical that your swimmers control their imagery so that they visualize only the desired outcome.

Visualization can be used in a variety of ways. It can be used to help a swimmer prepare for an upcoming meet or major competition. (Some coaches actually show their athletes pictures or videos of the pool and the surroundings where they will compete.) Imagery can greatly assist athletes who are learning a new skill or strategy. It helps them to become more familiar and comfortable with it before they attempt to physically perform the skill, thus helping to speed up the learning process. Visualization can be used to raise or lower an athlete's arousal level. You can increase your swimmers' confidence by asking them to visualize their past most successful experiences—as a kind of mental personal highlight film. After they image their past successes, have them visualize an upcoming meet so that the confidence, excitement, and happiness are transferred to the future event. (If swimmers have videotapes of their swims, they can create highlight films by splicing together their most outstanding swims.) It can be additionally beneficial to add the music of the swimmer's choice to this video and to have the athlete listen to that music prior to competing.

Many athletes use visualization to detect or overcome errors in technique. Visualization can and should be used to help your swimmers attain the various goals they have set for themselves, and it can be used during practice to prepare for a goal set. Visualization can be used to help speed up recovery from an injury or illness, usually with biological or fantasy imagery. Physiologically, it has been shown that imagery creates measurable amounts of contraction in the muscles used to perform the imagined movements. Consequently, a sick or injured swimmer who practices visualization is actually working his or her muscles to some degree. Athletes can also use visualization to see themselves staying healthy, training hard all through the season, and hitting their taper perfectly.

Some additional benefits of imagery are that it can be practiced equally well when the athlete is physically tired or well rested. It can be utilized when there is a problem with the facility and also as a change of pace during practice.

There are some guidelines your swimmers should follow when practicing visualization. First, relaxation should generally precede the use of imagery. The visualization should be desirable and believable, and the swimmer should expect the outcome of the imagery. Imagery must be practiced on a regular basis, preferably daily, if the swimmer is to receive the maximum benefit of the technique (see Coaches' Clinic 2.3).

COACHES' CLINIC 2.3: POOLSIDE VISIONS

One excellent way to use visualization is to take a few minutes before practice starts and have your swimmers actually visualize themselves going through the workout. Swimming good repeats, using good stroke technique, challenging themselves, encouraging their teammates, finishing the workout feeling tired but also happy and proud that they made the most of their opportunity to train. Visualization can also be used before goal-set swims to help prepare the athletes to meet their goal times.

Concentration

Concentration is the ability to focus on the relevant aspects of the swim for the duration of the event. There are basically two dimensions to concentration, width and direction. The width of attention can range from extremely broad, taking in and processing a vast number of cues, to incredibly narrow, where the focus is on a single cue. The direction of attention is either focused internally to thoughts, feelings, or bodily processes or externally on things outside the person in the environment. Consequently, there are four types of attention: broad internal, broad external, narrow internal, and narrow external.

A broad internal type of attention would be used by swimmers when deciding how to swim an upcoming race. They'd consider their past experiences, their current level of conditioning, where they are in their training cycle, and the nature of the competition to develop a strategy and race plan for the event. Swimmers would use a broad external focus before the competition when they look at the heat sheet and find out what heat and lane they are in, who they are swimming against, approximately what time they will compete, what the pool is like, and if there is a place nearby where they can warm up once the meet has started. A narrow internal focus involves visualizing the race, monitoring and adjusting one's arousal level before competing, or controlling one's pace during the event. Your swimmers would use a narrow external type of attention immediately before the race when they are focusing on the sound of the gun, or briefly during the race to look at you or the lap counter, or perhaps toward the end of the last lap of the race to focus on the touch pad.

Stress affects concentration in a variety of ways. It causes attention to involuntarily narrow and become more internally directed. For a swimmer, if attention is too narrowly or too internally focused it may cause problems, such as missing important cues, failing to process relevant information, or directing attention to inappropriate cues. Additionally, under stress the shifting of attentional style becomes more difficult, and it causes the swimmer to rely on her or his attentional strength. Obviously, a swimmer who is unable to shift attentional styles will experience difficulties. For instance, when athletes resort to their dominant style of attending, this can be beneficial in limited aspects of the performance—a dominant style that is narrow external would likely give the swimmer a great start—but they would probably not be able to monitor or adjust their pace very well throughout the race. Consequently, athletes who are stuck in their dominant style will generally find their overall performance impaired.

A swimmer whose dominant style is a broad internal focus will most likely overanalyze. For example, suppose that before and during a butterfly race the swimmer is thinking: "Am I doing the stroke right? Are my hands entering in front of my shoulders? Am I getting a good catch? Should I press out further? I wonder if my timing is okay? Am I breathing in the right place?" This swimmer is attempting to focus on so many different things that he or she could not possibly swim the stroke very well.

Athletes with a broad external dominant style will fail to analyze, because they are too busy reacting to the situation. Often they repeat the same mistakes over and over because of lack of analysis. A common example of this is swimmers who consistently go out with the field and then end up dying and swimming a terrible time rather than determining their own pace and swimming their own race.

Athletes whose attentional strength is narrow internal tend to become too locked into their own ideas, thoughts, and feelings. During a race, it is very detrimental for a swimmer to focus on the fatigue or pain she or he is experiencing.

Finally, when narrow external is the overriding attentional style, the swimmer tends to lack flexibility and fails to adjust to a changing environment. This attentional style is exemplified by the athlete who is seeded third in the finals and believes that if she races and beats the top seed, she will win the event. Consequently, when the race begins, this swimmer directs all of her attention to defeating the first-place qualifier, only to find out that the swimmer in Lane 8 has finished first.

Top athletes use all four types of attention and develop the ability to shift back and forth to the most appropriate attentional style throughout their races (see Coaches' Clinic 2.4). These are skills which can be developed by athletes at all levels. Awareness of the different types of attention and how they can be utilized is the first step in improving the ability to concentrate.

COACHES' CLINIC 2.4: TWO-MINUTE DRILL

One exercise that can be used to develop and improve concentration skills is the 2-minute drill. This technique would be implemented during practice when there is a general lack of concentration and the workout is going badly. Call everyone together and say that things aren't going well and that you want to see things turned around—so, for the next 2 minutes you want all athletes to give their undivided, complete, and total attention to their swimming. The athletes begin their swim. Two minutes later you blow the whistle, and everyone stops and comes together. Ask them what they did to become more focused on their swimming. Then the athletes will relate their various methods for focusing, and you can encourage them to use these methods more often, as well as trying some of their teammates' methods.

Self-Talk

Whether they are aware of it or not, individuals carry on a silent conversation with themselves throughout most of the day. This internal dialogue can actually direct thoughts and behaviors. Self-talk is like a self-fulfilling prophecy; by spending so much time thinking about something, individuals can actually make it come true. Positive self-talk has an extremely beneficial effect on performance because it increases self-confidence and helps the individual remain calm and in control. Negative self-talk, however, hinders achievement by causing an increase in anxiety and a decrease in motivation and self-confidence. Most people are not even aware of their self-talk, let alone the effect it is having on their daily lives. Consequently, it will be helpful for you to have your swimmers monitor their self-talk. They should actually keep a diary or log of their self-talk before, during, and after competition and practice. This will help your swimmers discover the situations and circumstances that produce positive and negative self-talk.

Another method of obtaining information about self-talk is retrospection. This involves thinking about and visualizing previous competitions. The swimmer should include best and worst performances and attempt to identify the content and frequency of self-talk in each situation. By using retrospection and self-monitoring, your swimmers will be able to identify the positive and negative aspects of their self-talk and begin to change the negative self-talk.

One method of dealing with negative self-talk is called thought stopping, which involves briefly focusing on the negative thought and then using a "trigger" to stop or interrupt the unwanted thought and clear the mind. The trigger may be simply saying *"Stop!"* or creating the image of a stop sign in front of the eyes, or snapping the fingers. The trigger may be auditory, visual, or kinesthetic. The choice of a trigger may depend upon the swimmer's predominant style of learning. Most importantly, the trigger must feel natural and comfortable to the swimmer and be used consistently. Once the negative thought has been stopped and the mind has been cleared, a positive thought should be inserted into the mind. Some athletes, however, find it unrealistic or unbelievable to go directly from a negative to a positive thought, so initially they could insert a positive neutral thought, which is a pleasant or happy thought unrelated to the particular sport situation. ("Gosh, it's a beautiful day.") Or they could utilize a positive corrective thought, which is a thought that attempts to undo the negative thought. Negative thought: "I hope I don't false start." Positive corrective thought: "When I get up on the blocks, I am going to keep my weight on my heels."

Initially, have your swimmers practice thought stopping during workouts. When a swimmer recognizes a negative thought, she or he should say "Stop" (or whatever cue she or he has picked) out loud. This will indicate to you that the swimmer is working on the new skill. After your swimmers begin to master this, have them say "Stop" to themselves. Another way to practice thought stopping is by using imagery. After they have practiced thought stopping during workouts and by using imagery, your swimmers should be ready to begin using it during competition.

A second method of dealing with negative self-talk is to refute it or actually build a case against the negative statement. For example, "I can't make 10 × 100 on 1:20":

- "Two weeks ago I made seven of them, and now I'm in much better shape."
- "I've increased my weights, so I know I'm stronger now."
- "I've been working on my turns lately, and I know they are better, so that will help my time."
- "If I want to improve, I know I have to push myself through this set."
- "Kathy made this set last time, and my best time is better than hers."
- "I've made 20 × 100 on 1:30, so I can do this."

A third method of dealing with negative self-talk is to use positive self-talk more frequently. Positive self-talk is a great help to swimmers when they are learning new skills or breaking bad habits. Self-talk is beneficial for creating and sustaining moods and effort levels during practice and competition. Self-talk can focus and direct attention, and the use of positive self-talk has been shown to increase athletes' self-confidence. Some athletes benefit from taping themselves making positive statements about their swimming and listening to it when they wake up and before they fall asleep. Some athletes like the tape to include their coach or teammates who are important to them making positive statements about their swimming.

Coaching Effectiveness

It is important that you serve as a role model for your athletes. Good coaches are first and foremost good communicators: They communicate in their attitude and appearance as well as in their training schedules and skill demonstrations. Good coaches understand swimming, the human mind and body, planning and preparation, and individual differences. They communicate their knowledge, understanding, and concern to their swimmers.

You also need to be an effective teacher, explaining the season plan to your athletes at the beginning of the season and discussing the why and how of training, stroke mechanics, starts, turns, and race strategies. You should answer any questions athletes may ask and try to refrain from the authoritarian response "Because I said so." You should not claim to know it all, and you should be willing to listen and remain open to new ideas and concepts.

It is important for athletes to understand why they swim different types of sets and to believe that these are beneficial. Consequently, you need to explain and convince your swimmers of the importance of various sets. However, there needs to be a mutual trust between you and your swimmers, and sometimes they must take your word for it and persevere.

You must be flexible and understanding, realizing that swimming is important to your swimmers but that occasionally family, school, or social events take precedence. If you have this flexibility, your swimmers will not feel as if they are always missing out on things because of their sport.

You must have a high degree of ego strength and self-confidence so that you do not make your swimmers dependent on you. Educate your swimmers about their swimming and teach them personal responsibility, so that they don't become dependent on you to train or perform well. Your swimmers should have every reason to believe that, if you were to leave, they could train and swim well with another coach.

It is also important for you to treat your athletes consistently. It's human nature for you to pay the most attention to your best swimmers, so you need to be mindful of this and careful that you treat your athletes equally. You need to make every one of your swimmers feel that he or she is extremely important to you. Following a race, it is the swimmer who performed poorly who most needs a word from you, not the one who just won the event or had her or his best time.

You should also be careful about the types of touching you use with your athletes, especially male coaches of junior and senior high school females, or female coaches of adolescent males. It is very common for adolescents to develop "crushes," and the meaning of a touch can easily be misconstrued. Therefore, you would be wise to limit physical contact to hands, arms, and shoulders with adolescent athletes.

PUTTING SPORT PSYCHOLOGY TO WORK FOR YOU

As coach, you will get the most from sport psychology by practicing the psychological techniques presented in this chapter until you can apply them without having to think about it. Focus on using effective communication and teaching swimmers about goal setting, imagery, self-talk, and relaxation to optimize their motivation, arousal, and concentration and to prevent burnout.

Sport psychology principles work best when utilized in a consistent, continual, and concrete approach. Your athletes can benefit the most from a program that teaches them psychological principles and then applies them during the practice session. You can plan a number of short sessions during the season for instructing your athletes. Suggestions for such a progression of sessions appear in Coaches' Clinic 2.5.

It is important to start mental training at the onset of the season. Initially, you should take time out of practice to introduce all of the aspects of mental training. During these sessions your athletes should keep a notebook that they will use throughout the season to record what they learn, what works best for them, and how they can apply it. Require your athletes to practice these mental techniques on a daily basis. This can be done at various times such as during stretching or circuit training, between sets, or at home. By practicing these techniques on a daily basis, the athletes will not only become more competent in the various mental skills, but their workouts will improve and they will be better prepared to utilize these techniques during competition.

Mental skills training should attempt to fit into the periodization and cycles that occur in physiological training. It should be used to assist or complement the physical training. For example, during the heaviest work load, place an emphasis on relaxation training to help the athlete recover more quickly and completely from the workout. During the taper phase, stress self-talk; the things that athletes say to themselves regarding their taper are critical to performance. Suggestions for a progression of mental training sessions appears in Coaches' Clinic 2.5.

COACHES' CLINIC 2.5: PSYCH SESSIONS

Session 1: Psychology and Peak Performance
- Explain the connection between mind and body.
- Have athletes take some time to visualize two of their best past performances.
- List and discuss psychological aspects of peak performance.
- Ask athletes to characterize their performances, and identify their own peak performance state.

Session 2: Communication
- Explain the importance of verbal and nonverbal communication.
- Explain the traits of a good listener.
- Run the rumor mill (Coaches' Clinic 2.1).

Session 3: Goal Setting
- Explain the goal setting process.
- Take time with each athlete to set mutually agreed upon goals (practice and competition) for the season.
- Write down all the goals you agreed upon and have athletes post them in a conspicuous spot.
- Develop an action plan to achieve the goals, including a goal-set swim.

Session 4: Arousal
- Introduce arousal and the inverted U theory.
- Outline symptoms of overarousal and its negative effects.
- List and demonstrate relaxation techniques, such as breath control and progressive relaxation.

Session 5: Imagery
- Explain visualization—using all senses and emotions.
- Teach correct technique for imagery: favoring internal over external perception, making images believable, and using imagery regularly.
- Outline the uses of imagery: learning a new skill, correcting a performance error, preparing for a competition, fine-tuning arousal, and instilling confidence.
- Have swimmers take a minute to visualize a perfect performance in a goal-set swim, then send them in to swim!

Session 6: Concentration
- Explain the different types of concentration: broad-narrow, internal-external and the appropriate use of each type.
- Explain how stress tends to narrow and internalize attention.
- Outline the pitfalls of different dominant attentional styles.
- Run the 2-minute drill to teach students about strategies for improving concentration.

Session 7: Self-Talk
- Explain what self-talk is and what effects it has.
- Have athletes monitor their self-talk by starting to keep diaries and using retrospection.
- Outline ways to stop negative self-talk: thought-stopping, refutation, and positive self-talk.

KEYS TO SUCCESS

- Physical and mental training are needed for peak performance.
- Mental skills, like physical skills, need to be practiced regularly to develop and maintain proficiency.
- Mental skills learned to benefit sport performance can also enhance other aspects of an individual's life.
- Listening is an active process that requires a high degree of concentration.
- All messages should be clear, consistent, and direct.
- Intrinsic motivation is the most powerful and desirable source of motivation.
- Set goals for competition and practice, develop a realistic plan that is free of sabotage, and evaluate goals regularly.
- Burnout is an avoidable condition.
- Muscle tension inhibits performance.
- Athletes can decrease their arousal levels by using a relaxation technique.

- Vivid, controlled, positive imagery can be used in a variety of ways to improve performance.
- Monitoring and adjusting attentional focus throughout the race is essential for peak performance.
- Self-talk may enhance or inhibit performance; therefore, it is essential to develop and maintain positive self-talk.
- You must be a positive role model.

REFERENCES AND RESOURCES

Martens, R. (1987). *Coach's guide to sport psychology.* Champaign, IL: Human Kinetics.

Nideffer, R.M. (1985). *Athletes' guide to mental training.* Champaign, IL: Human Kinetics.

Orlick, T. (1986a). *Coaches' training manual to psyching for sport.* Champaign, IL: Human Kinetics.

Orlick, T. (1986b). *Psyching for sport.* Champaign, IL: Human Kinetics.

Biomechanics: Teaching Swimmers to Swim Correctly

John Leonard
Executive Director
American Swimming Coaches Association

Two 7-year-old girls in Southern California started in a swim-lesson program together. They were close friends and good athletes who played a number of sports. Each learned to swim that summer, and by the end of July their teacher suggested that they join the club swim team for the summer league championships. They both did, and Sally won the 25-yard freestyle. Susie swam a little more slowly, but still enjoyed herself. They both enjoyed the swim meet and the ribbons and the attention from the older swimmers and their parents enough to want to swim on a team that winter.

Sally, because she won the 25 free in the summer, was put with the age-group team, where initially she was the slowest person in the group. The coach thought Sally had a lot of potential. Her size was also an advantage, as she stood a head taller than all the other 8-and-unders, including her friend Susie. Meanwhile, Susie was put into the novice group, which met only on Monday, Wednesday, and Friday for an hour. She was sad to be separated from Sally, but she liked her new friends and liked the way her coach spent time slowly teaching them to dive from the starting blocks and let them work on all four of their strokes.

As the season progressed, Sally started to win all the 8-and-under events in Southern California and dominated the freestyle events, even breaking a Southern California record by a swimmer who had later gone on to win an Olympic medal. Her parents were very proud of her and began giving her a dollar each time she swam a best time. They started to hear from the other parents that Sally might even some day be an Olympian herself. They asked the coach about this, and he smiled and said, "We'll see!" Sally was really enjoying swimming.

In the next to last meet of the season, Susie finally won her first ribbon, for the 100 backstroke, when she passed a much larger girl in the last 10 feet of the race. She was as happy that for once she had not spent half the race running into the lane lines, as she was about the ribbon. Her parents were also pleased for her, and the coach reminded her that she had kept her head still for the entire race, and that was why she had swum straight. She swam three other strokes in that meet, and though she didn't win another race, she went best times in each and felt good about her swimming. By the end of the season, she had progressed to the top of the novice team.

In the next 3 years both Sally and Susie continued to swim. Sally became an age-group star in Southern California, was nationally ranked in the top 10 in her age group for freestyle, and was being hailed as a potential top senior swimmer. By the time she was 11, she was beginning to train several times a week with the senior team, was doing many yards in workouts, and was physically capable of work far beyond her years. She really liked freestyle, and though she had some unusual stroke quirks, her parents knew that she was very talented, and those things were just her individual style. She was so good in freestyle, they really wanted her to swim just those events, rather than tire herself out in meets trying to swim butterfly, breaststroke, and backstroke as well. Sally was a star.

Susie had moved up to the age-group team and had paid attention to the coach and all the skills he taught the team. She hadn't grown much and was still kind of small, especially compared with her friend Sally. She noticed immediately that when they stood next to one another, they were physically very different now. Sally looked more like the teenagers, and Susie was obviously more like the 10-year-olds. She swam all four strokes in practice and in meets and paid attention to all the little things that made the stroke perfect. She liked the idea of doing things perfectly, even if she wasn't very fast yet. Gradually, she did begin to place in races more frequently. She noticed that she seemed to do better in the longer races of the strokes. She still couldn't compete with the better swimmers in freestyle. Susie really liked swimming and all there was to learn about it.

Between the ages of 12 and 15, some startling changes occurred. Sally worked harder and harder, attended every workout, and did every bit of work the coach put before her. She got faster. But as time went on, she noticed that she was improving less and less. She also was winning less and less. That was disturbing. She really preferred the shorter sprints, because when she swam the 200 free and longer, she couldn't seem to win as easily, and she struggled more and more as the race went on. Her coach also noticed that she was not winning as often, as did her parents. Everyone urged her to "work harder." She thought she was already working hard, which made this tough to understand. She was happy to discover that now her friend Susie was sometimes in the final heat of events with her, and that was nice—they were back together after all those years of swimming. She was still beating Susie all the time in freestyle, but in those few races when she swam backstroke, Susie could now beat her. In fact, Susie was regularly winning backstroke races across Southern California, and sometimes butterfly and IM races as well. Susie was more amazed at her body. She had grown about 6 inches in the last 2 years, and all of a sudden she had muscle on her arms and legs. That made it a lot easier to do the stroke drills she had been practicing since age 8, and it was really a terrific feeling to do easily those things she used to struggle to do. She still liked the little things, the technical things, the intellectual parts (as her coach said) about swimming. Susie was a very good swimmer. She was technically excellent. Her longer races were great, because when everyone else got tired at the end, she was able to keep her stroke together and stay efficient. The older she got, the better she was able to sprint.

Susie and Sally made their first National Junior Olympic Meet in the same year. A year later, Susie made senior nationals, and 2 years after that she qualified for the USA Olympic team in the 200 backstroke. Sally finaled in the 50 free in her second National Junior Olympic Meet and was one of the better high school sprinters in Southern California, but she gradually got to the point where she really didn't want to race over 100 yards very much. When it came time for college, the year Susie made the Olympic team, Sally got her college scholarship. It was for half tuition to a school in the Midwest that had finished in the top 15 at the NCAAs the year before. She and her parents watched the Olympics on TV and were thrilled for Susie when she won a silver medal and a gold in the relay. Two years later, Sally decided she had gone far enough in swimming, and she ended her career after the conference championships. A decade later, she came back to swimming, and she is now learning how to swim backstroke, breaststroke, and butterfly for fun in Masters competition.

WHY BIOMECHANICS IS IMPORTANT

The story I just told is true. And it illustrates the importance of learning swimming technique. The same story is played out in swimming pools and communities across the nation every day. Swimming is technique limited. Long-term success, satisfaction, and progress all require working to perfect technique. In youngsters, early size, strength, and maturity may result in initial competitive success, but as maturation proceeds, the differential between athletes becomes technique, and then training.

The faster the athlete becomes, the more critical the aspect of technique becomes. Teaching the athlete to swim properly to start with is the most important thing you can do to aid performance, and constant attention to technical details is the price of continued improvement.

Swimming is an unusual sport because the coach must be the "eyes" of the athlete. Vision and body perception are extremely limited for athletes while they are swimming, and it is up to the coach to provide accurate feedback on technical performance. Without this feedback the athlete is in essence swimming "blind" and will have a difficult time "feeling" the mistakes and flaws that exist.

Although the "art" of teaching the required skills takes many years of effort to acquire, the science of biomechanics is more straightforward, and by understanding just a few principles, you can create an adequate "tool kit" to teach and correct strokes for most swimmers. Through the experience of working with many swimmers in an intense effort to improve their strokes, you will gradually develop the art of recognition and correction that makes a coach a true professional.

Our aim in this chapter is to provide that basic tool kit, while reminding you that the potential for developing new and "specialized" tools is unlimited. The knowledge we benefit from today is the result of coaches like yourself, who seek and find new tools for us all to use. Read this chapter with the mind of a toolmaker.

BIOMECHANICAL CONCERNS IN SWIMMING

A coach has two major concerns with biomechanics: the reduction and limitation of resistance, and the improvement of the delivery of power. We shall first address the question of resistance.

Resistance is the greatest limiting factor in improving performance. This is because, as speed increases one unit, resistance increases at a rate 4 times greater. This disproportionate increase is what ultimately decides how fast a given performer can swim. You must spend considerable time with both your elite and your developing swimmers to reduce resistance. Teaching proper techniques to minimize resistance early in their learning progression greatly improves your swimmers' chances for later success.

Improving the delivery of power is also very important. The muscles provide the contractile force to move the levers that move the body through the water. Good teaching in biomechanics can provide the most effective use of the force that any individual can generate.

Focus on removing the limitations of resistance and maximizing the muscular force generated by the athlete. Clearly the quest to lessen resistance while maximizing the delivery of power approaches an art on the part of the coach.

Reducing and Limiting Resistance: How Do We Do It?

There are three major types of resistance that you must be concerned with, and we shall look at each in turn. You can teach your swimmers to control each to varying degrees.

Form Resistance

Form resistance is both the simplest and the most important kind of resistance, because the athlete has the most control over it. Simply put, form resistance is the amount of difficulty a body has in slipping through the water. A block shape offers more resistance to moving through the water than a spear. Your task is to help your swimmers shape themselves more like spears than blocks.

The possibilities here are limited by actual body shape and by the positioning and orientation of the body during the stroke. Some swimmers are blessed with exceptionally fine spear-shaped bodies, whereas others are limited by the block shape they are genetically disposed toward. Properly done, weight control can make some headway in maximizing the potential of the existing basic shape.

The major impact can be made by the positioning and orientation of the body. You and the swimmer should always be conscious of what head-on profile the swimmer's body presents to the water (see Coaches' Clinic 3.1). The task is to make this profile as small as possible. Ideally, the body lines up directly behind the profile presented by the swimmer's head and shoulders as they proceed down the pool.

COACHES' CLINIC 3.1: RECOGNIZING RESISTANCE

Ask the swimmer to compare and contrast the feel of the stroke while presenting both streamlined and resistant profiles to the water. Having swimmers simply pushing off the wall in various body positions is the simplest way to illustrate the dramatic effect good body position has on speed. Asking the swimmer to raise the head position while not increasing the kick proportionately will also immediately demonstrate the principle of form resistance. One good exercise for looking at form resistance is to pair up swimmers and have each look at the other under water from the front and side and coach each other on possible improvements in streamlining.

Surface Resistance

Surface resistance is the friction between the water and the various surfaces on the swimmer that contact the water. Swimmers and coaches have devised a number of ways to significantly reduce this form of resistance, including these:

- "Slick" swimsuits—The progress of competitive swimming attire throughout the 20th century has been remarkable, from the suits of the 1910s that featured skirts, full-length arms and legs, and the male "long-underwear" look, to the skintight, minimalist styles of the 1990s. Fabric, too, has seen a remarkable evolution from water absorbent materials to high-tech, super-slick plastics that completely shed water, so competitors carry no extra water with them at all. Suits are a prime consideration in reducing surface resistance.

- Shaving—In addition to the ritual significance of the swimmer's shaving before major meets, removing body hair does reduce the adherence of water molecules to the body. The physics of this reduction contributes, but the "psych" of the act of shaving as a team ritual probably is at least as important as the time reductions that result. There may also be increases in proprioceptive acuity with a shaved body, but this is as yet unproven.
- Caps—Water-repellent caps contain the hair in a slick, nonresistive surface to reduce resistance.
- Body lotions—Recent developments of high-tech, graphite-type solutions to apply to the body also may prove to reduce surface resistance. Various kinds of body oils and lotions have been used for this purpose for years, and they are perfectly legal unless deemed "excessive" by the referee.

Over the past 2 decades, swimmers have increasingly experimented with both increasing and decreasing surface resistance to make training more challenging and competition more specialized. They may choose to wear baggy suits and panty hose and keep long hair on body, face, and head in training, then gradually apply the improvements in different combinations as the intensity of the season heats up in more and more important meets. The same swimmer who shows up for a dual meet in midseason in a 5-year-old baggy suit (or two suits), with full body hair, a beard, and no cap, will appear at the Olympic trials in a plastic suit of almost invisible size, with plastic cap or shaved head, and a shaved body covered with the latest in body lotions. He can look like (and perform like) two totally different athletes in his effort to reduce surface resistance. Swimmers have many tools in their kits to work on this limitation.

Wave Resistance

Of the three types of resistance that you and your swimmers must be concerned with, wave resistance is least controllable. Essentially, it is a function of pool design and equipment usage.

Deep pools are faster than shallow pools, because the waves generated by the swimmers go deeper and dissipate, rather than ricocheting off the shallow bottom and bouncing the swimmer around on the surface. Pools with effective gutter systems absorb the wave energy and provide smooth, still water for the competitors. Quality lane lines provide the same wave dissipation capacity and help make for a "fast" pool.

Naturally, you and your swimmers have no control over these factors, other than insisting that the competition be conducted in the best quality facility available.

Let's look now at the other side of the fence, the delivery of power and how to effectively improve it.

Improving the Delivery of Power: How Do We Do It?

There are two ways to deliver power to the swimming stroke. The first is by effectively applying the lift force. The second is by applying the drag force. In real swimming conditions, the two forces interact at various points in each stroke to produce what we call the resultant force. The resultant force is nothing more than the combination of lift and drag in various contributing ratios. In effect, the resultant force can be best described as the force generated by lift and drag acting together. In determining how to help your swimmers go faster, your major emphasis should be on improving lift force; considerations of drag force are secondary. The reasons for this priority are described below.

The Lift Force

The lift force is the most significant concept for you to thoroughly understand in biomechanics. This is because many things can be done to improve its ability to work for the swimmer, and because most of the propulsion an athlete can generate comes from this force. Improvements in lift force are what turn poor swimmers into good swimmers, and good swimmers into great swimmers (see Coaches' Clinic 3.2).

The Drag Force

One of the confusing points in biomechanics is the unfortunate name, *drag force*. It sounds like drag force is a function of resistance to progress through the water. This is incorrect. Drag force actually is a measure of the force generated by the hand and arm actually moving water molecules backward in the water. It is an actualization of Newton's third law, of action/reaction. We push water back and generate force in a direction 180 degrees from that pushing action. Until the late 1960s the assumption was that this was what moved us forward in the water. Scientific research since that time has shown us that propulsion is much more complicated than that.

In practical terms, the most important thing to remember about the drag force is that there is very little we can do to improve its application in any swimmer. A swimmer's hand/arm configuration is capable of moving just so many water molecules, and no more. Unless a swimmer increases in

COACHES' CLINIC 3.2: KEYS TO LIFT PROPULSION

There are only a few key points to understand in regard to the lift force.

Point 1

Recognize that the shape of the human hand or foot is similar to that of an airplane wing or propeller. It is thicker on one side, then tapers to a thin edge. It is flat on one side (palm) and curved on the other (back of hand). It tapers from its attachment at the wrist (or the body of the plane) to the fingertips (end of the wing).

Point 2

Water (or air) passes around the wing at different speeds—faster over the curved surface, slower under the flat side. At any given instant, there are thus fewer water molecules above the wing than below it, creating a relative vacuum above the wing. The wing is "sucked" into that vacuum, and lift force occurs in the direction of the curved surface of the wing. Another way to look at this is to say that lift force is applied at a 90-degree angle to the flow (in this case, flow of water over the leading edge of the wing). In practical terms, you should remember that phrase: *Force is generated at a 90-degree angle to the flow*. It takes practice and thought to always recognize where the flow over the leading edge is, and thus where the lift force is being applied.

Point 3

The faster the flow, the greater the lift force. This is another way of saying that the acceleration of the wing produces greater lift force. The wing (hand) is accelerated by applying greater muscular force in the movement. Thus, the improvement of strength interacts very effectively with improvement in stroke technique and the lift force.

Point 4

The wing's angle of attack is critical to the successful application of force. As illustrated, when the lead edge of the hand is "flat," or straight on into the flow, lift does occur, but it occurs much more strongly when the hand is pitched slightly "upward" to improve the lift factor. (This can be simply demonstrated by "playing" with your hand in the windstream out the window of a moving car. A flat approach to the wind will not produce the same lift as a pitched hand, but too much pitch will simply result in the hand being blown backward—this is the "stall point.")

body size (or she or he is able to move the water faster, through greater muscular power), there is not much you can do to improve drag force. As your swimmers gain strength, the application of it to the lift force is actually much more productive.

Your job is to devise teaching methods to improve your swimmers' ability to create more lift force in each stroke. As the hand or foot moves through the stroke pattern, there are various interactions (resultant forces) of the lift force and the drag force, each contributing in various degrees to the total propulsion of the body. Our next section discusses practical ways to analyze your swimmers' strokes.

Practical Stroke Analysis

It is important for you to understand the scientific basis for propulsion and resistance, but it is even more vital that you be able to translate this knowledge into useful teaching tools for your swimmers.

The Three-Dimensional Stroke

Using lift and drag forces in concert produces propulsion. The concept of lift implies that a sculling or cutting motion, with one edge of the hand (thumb side) leading, gives the most effective "wing" to produce force. The task, then, is to move this leading edge through as much water as possible. This means that the hand must move through the width and the depth dimension (see Figures 3.1a and 3.1b). When we analyze the hand position of successful swimmers, we see that lift actually allows the athlete to anchor the hand and pull the body past it—or in the case of the truly gifted athlete, the hand actually moves forward through the water, and the body moves past the forward-moving hand. This can be observed by watching the hand entry of gifted swimmers against the background of the lane lines. The hand actually exits in front of where it entered. This is only logical. If the hand moved "backward" through the water, how would the body move forward? So in actuality, a forward-moving hand is pulling the body past. The result also shows a hand movement that includes the length dimension of the body. So the three dimensions a swimmer must have in all strokes are length, width, and depth.

Look for the appropriate changes in each dimension of the stroke. A two-dimensional stroke will not provide the propulsion available from the full use of three dimensions. In various strokes, at various levels of fatigue, individual swimmers will "lose" the ability to move through one or more dimensions. Improvement comes from maintaining stroke discipline to use all three dimensions. Learn to look for length, width, and depth changes in all strokes when analyzing your athletes, and teach

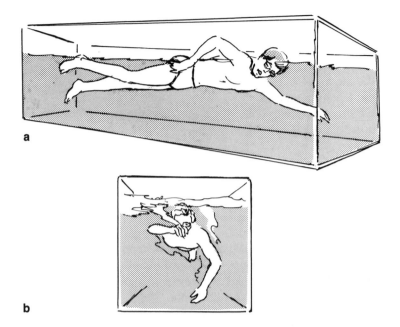

Figure 3.1 Rather than cuing on the two-dimensional waterline, swimmers should visualize themselves swimming in a long rectangular box with (a) length and (b) width and depth.

them the language you will use to discuss the needed changes with them. Later in this chapter, we will explain the appropriate changes in each stroke in terms of length, width, and depth.

Acceleration

The other aspect to observe when teaching or correcting strokes is to notice that the wing must accelerate to provide improved propulsion. Generally, acceleration increases from the extremity of the stroke to the center of the movement, and then accelerates again to the "end" of the in-water portion of the stroke. We'll look at this carefully, also, in our study of each stroke. In constructing a three-dimensional stroke, remember to consider

- length,
- width, and
- depth

and remember that the principle of acceleration must be observed in the motion of the limb through the three dimensions.

Teaching and Correcting Strokes

The factors involved in good teaching and correction of strokes include

- the language of the stroke,
- the teaching environment,
- where and how to view the stroke, and
- understanding individual variations in technique.

We'll now look at each of these.

Language of the Stroke

It is important for you to remember that your swimmers will form "word pictures" of their strokes in their minds, and they will perform the strokes in conformance with these "word pictures." Your role is to place the correct word picture of the stroke into the swimmer's mind. Provide a verbal description of the stroke, with the same language usage each time, and teach and correct with this consistent language. Swimmers learn by many methods, including the verbal, visual, and kinesthetic. Their verbal understanding of the stroke is vital in contributing to their pictures of what they are accomplishing in the water. Later, when we discuss each stroke, we will provide a sample word picture of each stroke, but you should become proficient in providing your own preferred picture. Teaching your swimmers to tell you about their strokes verbally can provide real clues to where they are experiencing difficulties. Sometimes verbal correction can even aid physical correction.

The Teaching Environment

Where and how you teach is critical to your success in teaching biomechanics, and a full discussion of this topic is beyond the scope of this chapter, but here are a few things to be aware of. First, there is a time and place for both group and individual teaching. Explanation and demonstration of the stroke are appropriate for group applications, and perhaps correction is best done individually. The use of group drills is good because your swimmers can see peers performing the skill as they work to perfect their own. Drills also work well individually as a method of "overcorrection." Drilling a segment of a stroke seems to be particularly effective in swimming, perhaps because swimmers have limited use of vision and hearing while they are in the water. Isolating movements may also be important.

Disciplined teaching environments, where the emphasis is on learning, are probably preferable when introducing new water skills, and some unstructured time to "experiment" is also important to help swimmers learn "feel" for the water. "Feel" is another way to describe how the athlete learns to use the lift principle in action. Free time and play, where the athlete must change direction sharply and rapidly, can really teach feel for the water. Water polo is excellent for this purpose. As in all good teaching, variety of methods plays a key role. The swimmer who fails to grasp something in a group may learn it best in an unstructured individual period of play. Others may need structured one-on-one time with you to make stroke corrections. Your challenge as a coach is to have a plan that provides all of these possibilities.

Looking at a Stroke

You also need variety. You cannot look at the same stroke from the side of the pool each day and see any new ways to improve it. You need to see the stroke from the side, from the front, from above, from below, and in combinations of all of those.

Get in the habit of climbing up on the diving board several times a week to see your swimmers from a height. Put on a suit and a scuba tank, and look at them from underneath. Use a mask, fins, and snorkel to see their strokes underwater. Watch them from every angle. Remember, you are looking for three-dimensional strokes. This means that you must be in a position to see from all dimensions.

Individual Variations in Stroke

Always remember, when teaching strokes, that you are dealing with individuals. Each athlete has personal strengths and weaknesses. Each has differing abilities in terms of flexibility, muscular strength, and endurance. One stroke will not work for everyone. Swimmers develop their personal "signature strokes" within the parameters of their own abilities. As a coach, your role is to provide the framework of the stroke for them to build on as they will. You have the unique charge of keeping your swimmers' "creativity" within reasonable bounds, where scientific principles of propulsion and limiting resistance are observed, while allowing them to develop their own styles in the water. The interaction of the two is where the artistic side of coaching emerges, and you have a most fascinating and involving job. Enjoy the challenge.

Now it is time to look at each of the four competitive strokes and discuss the scientific framework that we consider to be "state of the art" stroke mechanics today.

Stroke Mechanics

For each of the four competitive strokes, we begin with a structured verbal outline of the stroke, then follow with a discussion of some of the most important teaching points.

Freestyle

Body Position.   In freestyle, the body should ride as high in the water as possible while remaining relaxed. The head position helps determine the position of the body. In general, the water should be touching the head at the hairline. As the swimmer extends each arm forward, the body should roll onto that side (see Figure 3.2). In both freestyle and backstroke, tremendous efficiencies are gained by swimming the stroke predominantly on the side.

Figure 3.2   Correct body position for freestyle includes rolling onto the stroking side and positioning the head so the waterline meets the hairline.

Breathing Mechanism.   Air is exhaled underwater in either a steady or an explosive manner. The head turns to breathe as the hand passes under the waist and progresses past the thighs. The head returns to the forward-looking position before the recovery hand passes the waist on its way forward.

The Kick.   The kick is fast, fluid, and relaxed. It begins high up, in the butt and upper thigh muscles, and continues down to loose, flexible ankles. The kick is relatively narrow and should be just below the surface of the water.

The Pull.   The hand reaches out and enters the water on a line directly above the shoulder. The hand enters index finger first, with the palm of the hand pitched outward at about a 45-degree angle. The elbow is up high on the entry. The hand extends out in front of the head and deep into the water (see Figure 3.3). Then the elbow bends, and the hand sweeps up to the high point of the chest, with the thumb leading. As it does so, the elbow points to the side wall of the pool. Then the hand pushes through under the body, until the thumb passes the thigh.

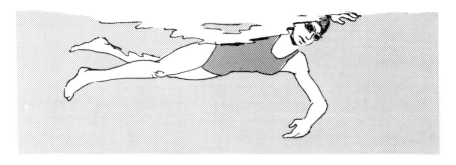

Figure 3.3 Just after entry, the hand extends in front of the head and moves deep before the elbow bend.

The Recovery.   As the thumb passes the thigh, the little finger turns and spins out of the water first. The body roll to the opposite arm aids in lifting the elbow, and the hand recovers close to the body, with fingertips close to the water. The back of the hand leads forward on the recovery (see Figure 3.4).

Figure 3.4 During recovery, the elbow stays high, and the back of the hand leads forward.

Discussion.   Modern research has concluded that body roll plays an enormous role in helping to create the hand and arm acceleration that generates speed. In particular, the role of the hips (hip speed through rotation) has recently received a lot of attention. The muscles of the hip area impart a "twisting" action to the entire torso that greatly helps to generate limb speed. The length component of this stroke is easy to recognize, as the hand enters above the head and exits by the hip. The depth component has the hand entering at the surface, driving deep first, then sweeping up to the chest, then sliding down to the hips, and finishing back at the surface. The width component begins at entry (shoulder width), then the hand moves to the center line of the body, then finally sweeps out past the hips. Changes in all three components are essential for fast swimming.

Backstroke

Body Position.   As in freestyle, the body must roll from side to side (see Figure 3.5). This greatly reduces the total resistance the body encounters as it progresses through the water. Also, you need to be concerned with the number of strokes taken in each race, as the total resistance to be overcome can be reduced significantly if the highly resistant "flat" position in each rotation can be minimized. In theory, the fewer strokes taken, the lower the total resistance that must be overcome.

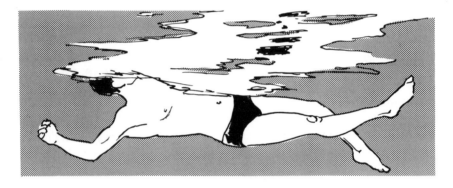

Figure 3.5   Significant body roll can lessen form resistance and improve speed.

Head Position.   This is a key in backstroke. The head position should be very, very still. The water should be just touching the ears when the swimmer is lying flat in the water, so the head and eyes are slightly inclined back toward the feet (see Figure 3.6). Some swimmers perform better with the head slightly farther back, depending on the event. General rule: The shorter the event, the higher the head; the longer the race, the farther back the head. The higher head position allows the legs a deeper and more propulsive kick, whereas the lower position is obviously more streamlined. Some trade-offs of power for streamlining, and vice versa, are possible by adjusting body position. In any case, the head must remain still.

Breathing Mechanism.   Contrary to appearances, one cannot simply breathe at will when on the back, for optimum results. Breathing affects the buoyancy of the body, and thus greatly affects the stroke. Best results are obtained by breathing in on one hand entry and out on the opposite hand entry. Inhalation on the dominant hand entry may be most effective

Figure 3.6   Correct head position keeps the waterline at the ears, eyes slightly inclined toward feet, and head very still.

in aiding power. The most important factor is establishing a breathing rhythm, as in the other strokes.

Kicking.   The backstroke kick is similar to freestyle in mechanics, but it is positioned somewhat deeper in the water. Unlike freestyle, where a number of timing mechanisms have been successful (six-beat kick, two-beat kick, etc.), the backstroke requires a steady six-beat kick to maintain body position and aid propulsion. Almost all good backstrokers are also excellent kickers.

The Pull.   The hand enters the water just outside a line drawn directly above the shoulder. The little finger leads on the entry. The first action is the hand knifing down through the water to a position wide and deep, with the elbow pointing toward the bottom of the pool. Driving the hand deep on this "catch" action is critical. The hand then sweeps "up and over" in an arc that is wide of the body. As the hand reaches the limits of its reach (wide of the body), the hand is accelerated up, across, and out past the hip. The palm of the hand faces the feet during this rapid acceleration. The thumb leads the hand out of the water (see Figure 3.7).

The Recovery.   The thumb exits first, and the recovery shoulder rolls up and out of the water as the opposite arm begins its catch. The recovery shoulder is rolled inward, clearing the water on a clean shoulder lift as the swimmer sights up the straight arm to the elbow, wrist, and fingers all in a straight line above the shoulder. Because the head remains still, the shoulder rolls toward the chin to reach this position in midrecovery.

Discussion.   As in freestyle, the body roll plays a key part in the effectiveness of the stroke. Length is again defined by entry above the shoulder, exit past the hip. Width begins with entry just outside the shoulderline,

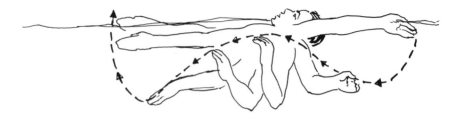

Figure 3.7   The complete pull of the backstroke, from the entry led by the little finger to the exit led by the thumb.

then the hand sweeps wide (and deep) and then sweeps inward once again to the hip. The depth change is very significant, beginning at the surface, driving deep, then sweeping upward and back down at full extension of the arm. Then the depth changes once more, as the hand is accelerated back to the surface past the hip. When swimmers become tired, the depth dimension is the one that is most usually lost in the mechanics of this stroke. Hand acceleration is from the wide-and-deep catch position through the over-the-top extension.

A second and very important acceleration occurs as the hand finishes the stroke past the hip. Maintaining a still head position is also a key, as the space between eye and recovery arm is an important perception that leads to hand entry in the proper position. Disruption of the proper perception by "wiggling" the head in any direction will throw off the entry position of the hand, a problem that is very difficult to compensate for later in the stroke. The backstroke thus requires a very disciplined approach to stroke mechanics.

Breaststroke

Body Position.   Success in breaststroke has been achieved with a great variety of styles. Most of the variations revolve around body position and at present include styles that best are described as "flat," "rolling" or "wave action," and "lift." Each style has its proponents and requires different physical characteristics in the athlete. As a young swimmer progresses in the stroke, some natural predispositions will emerge, and you should encourage the development of the body position that is natural for each individual.

Head Position.   Largely a function of the body position (style) selected, the head action is not pronounced in any but the lift style, where the chin is dropped so the face is looking at the bottom of the pool following the inhalation at the peak of the stroke and following kick. Breathing in all styles includes underwater exhalation, and inhalation at the top of the stroke.

The Kick. The breaststroke kick is propulsive and contributes much more to forward motion than do kicks in the other strokes. The action is as follows: The heels recover behind the buttocks, with the knees bending very significantly to do so (see Figure 3.8a). It is important to bring the heels to the butt, leaving the thighs essentially lined up with the belly, rather than drawing the knees under the body. The feet turn outward, with toes rotating to the outside as far as possible. The kick action is "back, down and around, and squeeze" (see Figure 3.8b). Kick width varies with the style being used, but most kicks are a comfortable width. Excellent propulsion can be found from both wide and narrow kicks, depending in part on the physical construction and strength of the individual. It is important to finish, or close the legs together, at the end of the kick.

a

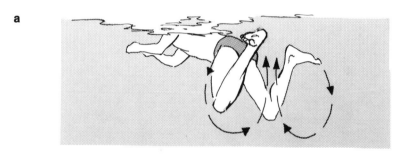

b

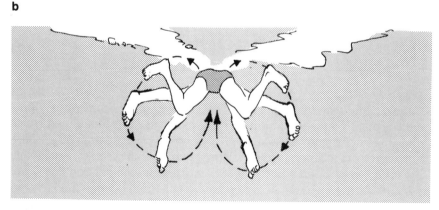

Figure 3.8 In the breaststroke kick, (a) the heels recover with significant knee bend, the feet approach the buttocks, and (b) the feet follow a circular kick pattern.

The Pull. This part of the stroke is becoming more uniform among all styles. The action is as follows: The hands recover with straight arms and hands extended and together, with thumbs down, hands pitched 45 degrees inward from the vertical (90 degrees from each other). The hands press wide (must press outside the elbows) and pitch up (see Figure 3.9). At the extreme width of the pull, the hands are vertical in the water, palms outward, thumbs down. From this position, the hands are swept inward and downward, while locking the elbows high, until the hands pass under the elbows. The hands accelerate greatly from the width of the stroke into the center. As they accelerate, the palms are pitched slightly out and backward. Individual variations of hand pitch will result in major differences in lift and propulsion, and your swimmers should experiment with these. As the hands pass under the elbows, the forearms are vertical in the water. As they pass under, the elbows may be forcefully squeezed together under the chin, creating a streamlined shape for the forward thrust of the kick.

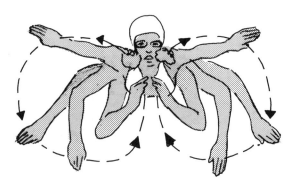

Figure 3.9   At the beginning of the breaststroke pull, the hands press wide at 45 degree angles (thumbs down) from the surface.

Timing.   Breaststroke timing is critical. One phrase to think of is "Kick, stretch, pull." The key point is to have the arms in a streamlined shape when the force of the kick is applied, and the legs in a streamlined position as the force of the arms is applied. When you teach this stroke, exaggerate this stretched position before the pull, because in competition the swimmer will shorten this stretch period and may tend to overlap the kick and pull to the detriment of the effectiveness of the whole stroke. At full speed, in mature, highly elite athletes, there is some small overlap of the kick and pull.

Discussion.   The length, width, and depth factors in breaststroke are critical. In the kick, the feet must travel through all three dimensions to be successful. The recovery starts narrow, then the propulsion must be both wide and changing in depth from shallow to deeper, and the crucial finish of the stroke with legs together once again changes the width.

In the pull, both width and depth again change dramatically: Depth is the dimension that swimmers usually neglect as they get tired and can no longer summon the strength to rotate the hands downward on the sweep. Instead, they tend to drop the elbows and slide the hands across the water, with palms facing down instead of out and backward. This has the effect of raising the body out of the water rather than forward. (Propulsion is found at a 90-degree angle to the flow of water over the leading edge of the hand.)

The length component is difficult to visualize, because all parts of the body actually move forward in the water. The feet actually "anchor" in the kick, and the body extends forward. The same occurs with the hands, as if one were opening a hole in a curtain and pulling the body through it.

Because this stroke is so complex, you would do well to teach basic skills of kicking, pulling, and timing, and then closely observe your swimmers for personal tendencies before settling on specific styles that suit the talents of the individuals.

Butterfly

Body Position.   The body position in the butterfly has a pronounced rolling action. As the hands enter the water, the hips must come up to the surface, sometimes breaking the surface. As the hips rise, the chest presses down into the water, giving an S shape from the hands on the surface to the lowered head and lower-still chest, back up to the hips at the surface. The legs trail back to the feet, which, having finished their downbeat, are deeper in the water (see Figure 3.10).

Head Position.   The back of the head generally aligns with the spine. As the hands finish the pull under the body, the chin stretches forward at the

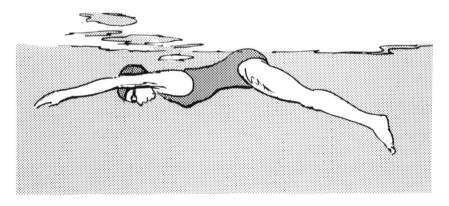

Figure 3.10   The body roll in the butterfly is pronounced, creating an S shape after the downbeat of the feet.

surface of the water for the inhalation. The exhalation is done underwater in either an explosive or a controlled manner.

The Pull.   The hands enter just outside the shoulder line, palms pitched out, thumbs and index fingers entering the water first, elbows tipped up slightly (see Figure 3.11). The hands then accelerate in a downward and inward sweep under the throat, where they almost touch. Elbows both point toward the side wall. The hands then press back and exit with the little finger "cutting" out of the water between the waist and the hips. There is acceleration from the entry to the center, and then again back past the hips. Your swimmers should try to "explode" the hands out of the water.

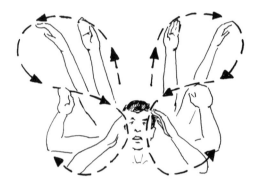

Figure 3.11   The curved path of the butterfly arm pull, seen from below.

The Recovery.   The arms are extended, relaxed, but relatively straight, and are brought forward over the surface of the water with the little fingers leading for as much of the recovery as possible. This helps to keep the shoulders rolled forward and in the water. The arms stay low and close to the surface on the recovery (see Figure 3.12). Sprint technique requires that the arms be "pulled" forward with the upper shoulder muscles for a faster recovery; longer fly swims have a ballistic recovery that is slower and less energy consuming.

The Kick.   The kick is really an extension of a properly done body roll through the stroke. The legs stay together, with toes pointed and relaxed. The effort should be to make the entire lower body into a giant swim fin. Retaining a full depth of kick during a race is important, and the amplitude of the kick contributes to its effectiveness. The fly kick is definitely propulsive, and there is significant knee bend on the downbeat. Thinking of forcing the back of the knee upward gives force to both the upbeat and the downbeat of the kick.

Figure 3.12   In the butterfly arm recovery, the little finger should break the water, the elbow remain relaxed, and the arm recover low over the water.

Discussion.   Teaching the body position, usually by a number of one-arm butterfly drills, is critical. The stroke is easily mastered if the timing of "Hands go in, buttocks go up" is felt and understood. It is impossible to place the kick in the "wrong" place in the stroke if this is accomplished. Properly done, the stroke flows through the water. Teaching breathing is also important, and keeping the chin firmly anchored near the surface instead of climbing out of the water to breathe is vital. Finally, most new butterflyers have a tendency to overkick the stroke, thus rapidly becoming tired and concluding that the stroke is difficult to swim. Nothing is farther from the truth. Teach body position and roll first, then arm action and pull, and then make the kick an extension of the body action.

PUTTING BIOMECHANICS TO WORK FOR YOU

Planning a complete program of stroke teaching for your team is the only way to ensure that you will cover all the necessary aspects of biomechanics. Repetition over a number of seasons is not only inevitable, but highly desirable, because not every athlete will be ready to learn all the points at one time. Each time you cover the stroke, some athlete will pick up a new point she or he is personally ready for. Do not fear being repetitious.

Start with verbal descriptions of the strokes. Sit your group down, explain how you would like each stroke to be swum in a "framework" form, and explain your acceptance of individual variation within that framework. Describe each stroke. Teach key stroke performance words. Then drill verbally on a daily basis, 5 to 10 minutes per day, as well as during the time between swimming sets, while the swimmers rest at the wall. Work daily to ensure that your athletes have an outstanding verbal and visual understanding of the strokes as you want them swum. Videotapes of outstanding swimmers playing constantly on the deck of your pool are excellent for this purpose.

Consider making your warm-up each day consist of stroke drills that require thought and effort to do each small part of each stroke perfectly. Use at least a few minutes each day to perfect a drill to use in workout. You should constantly be commenting, using the verbal outline you have established, to swimmers as they finish repeats and finish sets. This takes only a few seconds, and you can emphasize each teaching point for the swimmer. Teaching strokes is hard work, and you must actively pursue it. The rewards are unequaled. All great coaches are excellent stroke technicians.

Finally, you need a visual reinforcement. Create a notebook, or use a large bulletin board in the pool area, to create a series of pictures of each stroke that shows points you want to emphasize. Take these from swimming magazines and swimming books, and take your own of your own swimmers. Show the positive strokes you want. Keep a separate notebook that shows common stroke faults, in case you ever have a need to show a swimmer what he or she is doing incorrectly. Negative images are powerful, however, so use this device sparingly. The use of video to show great strokes has already been mentioned. Another use of video is to tape your own swimmers either above or below water, and review their strokes with them. Again, beware of creating strong negative images. This use of video does require advance planning for both practice and meets, and developing a system to do it effectively, and still keep yourself coaching, is a real challenge. If an assistant coach or a parent can do the actual taping, that can be helpful. There is no substitute for the coach reviewing the tape with the athlete, however, and that does take considerable time. Videotape for analysis purposes basically should be considered a one-on-one project. It can be a valuable addition to your kit of teaching tools.

KEYS TO SUCCESS

- **Teach swimmers that swimming is technique limited: Only with proper biomechanics can athletes reach their competitive potential.**

- **Emphasize biomechanics to reduce form resistance and find the proper balance of lift and drag forces.**

- **Make the complex simple: Reduce complex information into a form usable by your swimmers.**

- **Analyze each stroke as a three-dimensional movement, and watch for acceleration of the stroke to maximize lift force.**

- Plan your teaching process considering the language of the stroke, the teaching environment, where and how to view the stroke, and individual variations in technique.

- Plan your correction process using teaching aids such as posters, videotapes, notebooks, and bulletin boards, as available, to reinforce proper stroke mechanics.

- Make stroke work a daily priority in your program.

CHAPTER 4

Exercise Physiology: Proper Conditioning

Rick L. Sharp
Iowa State University

The temperature is well over 100 degrees and rising, oxygen pressure is already at critically low levels and continues to drop, ammonia has risen to nearly toxic heights, and pH is almost incompatible with life. Strange globular structures form and begin to engulf and digest the reed-like structures that comprise the landscape. The atmosphere crackles with charge as tiny explosions detonate in random patterns, vaporizing nearby boulder-like objects and throwing fragments in every direction. Clouds of carbon dioxide gas rise from bean-like pods scattered throughout the field of view. Clearly this chaotic dance of destruction signals impending collapse of this world.

No, this is not a scene from a recent science fiction movie. It is what you might see if you could look into the working muscles of a swimmer in the last lap of a 200-meter butterfly race. Indeed, the molecular and physiological events in muscle that make performance possible can create the most inhospitable environment this side of Mercury. Yet, as chaotic and destructive as these events might seem, they are ordered into perhaps the most complex and interactive machinery we will ever encounter. Solving the puzzle of this complex and alien world of exercising muscles is the goal of physiology. If we can unlock the secrets of this microscopic world, we can more effectively modify its environment to maximize training effects, prevent overtraining, and push back the barriers of human swimming performance.

WHY EXERCISE PHYSIOLOGY IS IMPORTANT

By itself, an understanding of the basic physiological responses to swimming races and training will not likely help you develop better swimmers. Physiology must be viewed as a tool. Left in the toolbox collecting dust, a hammer serves no purpose but to add to the burden the carpenter must carry to the job. Likewise, a coach can choose to be burdened by physiology or to make use of this potentially valuable implement. For example, you can use your knowledge of physiology to help determine the proper amount of rest between swims in interval training (see Coaches' Clinic 4.1). Such applications of physiology help eliminate some of the guesswork involved in coaching, increasing the probability that each conditioning drill in a practice session serves a specific purpose and achieves the desired outcome. This chapter is intended to help you gain some understanding of physiological principles of the conditioning process and to illustrate how you can put this information to use in designing training programs for your competitive swimmers.

Primary Roles

Of course, there are hundreds of different physiological systems that are affected by a single exercise bout, and many of these adapt to daily training to improve a swimmer's ability to resist fatigue, tolerate higher levels of training, and recover more quickly from strenuous exercise. It is beyond the scope of this chapter to cover all of these systems. Besides, a swimming coach does not need to completely understand all of these systems any more than a car driver needs to know everything about how a car works in order to be a good driver. But like the car driver, you

---

COACHES' CLINIC 4.1: RESTING FOR SUCCESS

Joe swims 10 × 25 freestyle all-out to work on developing his maximum sprint speed. The rest between each swim is 20 seconds. Joe is able to average 12 seconds on each of the first 4 swims, but his times get progressively slower on the last 5 or 6 swims, so that by the 10th swim his time is 13.5 seconds. The informed coach knows that to adequately stress the energy system used in sprinting, at least 1 minute of rest is required between swims to allow recovery of muscular stores of creatine phosphate. With the relatively short rest allowed on these swims, Joe's muscles become progressively depleted of this energy source and are thus forced to rely on the lactic acid energy system, which is the likely cause of the slower times. The next time this sprinting set is done, 1 minute of rest is allowed, and Joe can maintain his times at roughly 12 seconds for all 10 of the swims. This indicates that the energy system of sprinting is adequately recovered between swims and can be stressed again on each successive repeat.

---

should understand the primary roles associated with fuel efficiency and power production, and modifications that can be made to improve these factors.

Simply stated, the primary roles of physiology in swimming are to

1. provide muscle contractions to move the body, and
2. provide the energy necessary to sustain these contractions for various lengths of time.

Muscle Contraction

Muscle contracts as a result of an electrical stimulus provided by motor nerves. The signal that serves as this stimulus originates in the motor cortex of the brain and travels down along the spinal cord to the motor nerve and then down to the muscle cells that are served by that motor nerve. A complex series of events takes place in muscle that results in calcium ion being released in and around the contractile proteins of muscle. This calcium ion is considered the trigger for contraction and causes the shortening of these proteins with the energy supplied by the splitting of adenosine triphosphate (ATP). ATP is a molecule that cells produce from carbohydrate, fat, and protein used in energy metabolism. It acts like a battery, in that energy from these foods is transferred to a high-energy phosphate bond on ATP. Then when called upon to contract, the muscle cell breaks the phosphate bond to provide the energy for the work of contraction. In repetitive contractions, such as those involved in a 100-yard event, this process must be repeated thousands of times. The strength of the whole muscle contraction depends primarily on the number of these motor nerves and muscle fibers that are activated at the same time. Thus, anything that leads to a failure of any part of the neuromuscular ability to trigger the release of calcium will weaken the contractions. If some muscle fibers fail to recover fast enough to continue contracting, the nervous system will attempt to recruit additional motor nerves to prevent a loss of propulsion. As this occurs, the movements of the whole body become less coordinated (stroke mechanics deteriorate), and eventually the pace is slowed. This is defined as muscular fatigue. Events associated with this fatigue process include depletion of ATP in some muscle fibers, low muscular pH induced by accumulation of lactic acid within the muscle, and possible loss of functional abilities of some motor nerves.

Provision of Energy

Because ATP serves as the immediate energy source for the muscle contractions, it must be kept in constant supply to support repeated contractions. Human muscle depots of ATP are sufficient to sustain exercise for only about 1 second, however. Therefore, muscle must continually remanufacture ATP, ideally at the same rate at which it is being used. This resynthesizing process is made possible by at least three biochemical energy systems that operate within the muscle. Each of these systems can be thought of as energy factories driven by enzymes that harvest the potential energy contained in various fuels to re-form ATP.

Figure 4.1 is a diagram of the energy systems and of the muscle ATP pool. The diagram represents energy systems as tanks filled with liquid fuel. In each of the energy systems, the size of the tank and the quantity of fuel stored within are reflective of that energy system's total capacity to remanufacture ATP. In addition, each tank has a faucet, with the size of the faucet representing the maximum rate at which this energy system can process the fuel to form ATP. It should be immediately obvious that the faucet connected to the muscle ATP pool is the largest of the four. This means that the rate at which muscle is capable of using ATP for maximal exercise is far greater than any of the three energy systems could match if operating alone. Therefore, resynthesis of ATP during exercise is accomplished by relying on the combined actions of all three energy systems. (Some general characteristics of these systems are shown in Figure 4.2.)

The most rapidly responding energy system (the small tank with the large faucet in the figure) is the creatine phosphate system, which utilizes creatine phosphate (a high-energy molecule similar to ATP) that is stored

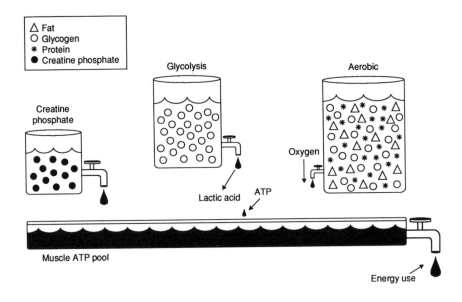

Figure 4.1   A model of the three energy systems of muscle that keep muscle stores of ATP constant during exercise.

	Creatine phosphate	Glycolysis	Aerobic
Fuel	Creatine phosphate	Muscle glycogen	Carbohydrate, fat, protein
Fuel availability	Limited	Medium	High
Maximum rate	Fast	Medium	Slow
Products	Creatine, ATP	Lactic acid, ATP	Carbon dioxide, ATP, water
Oxygen requirement	Only in recovery	Only in recovery	Exercise and recovery

Figure 4.2   Comparison of some characteristics of the three energy systems available to muscle for resynthesizing ATP.

within the muscle cells. As soon as the level of ATP in the muscle begins to fall, the enzyme creatine kinase (CK) starts cleaving the available creatine phosphate (i.e., the faucet opens). This reaction releases enough energy to resynthesize one molecule of ATP for every molecule of creatine phosphate. The product of this reaction, creatine, can be used after exercise to remanufacture creatine phosphate.

This system sounds almost ideal, because it does not require oxygen to be delivered from the lungs to the working muscle and does not depend on slow transport of fuel from other organs to the muscle. In addition, there is no reason to suspect that accumulation of the product creatine will cause any symptoms of muscular fatigue. In other words, it is a completely renewable energy source and burns clean. But unfortunately, this system is limited by the small supply of creatine phosphate stored in muscles. Humans store only enough creatine phosphate to sustain all-out exercise for maybe 5 to 15 seconds. However, because the fuel is stored within the muscle and only one chemical reaction is required to transfer the energy to resynthesizing ATP, this system is ideal for extremely short, high-intensity swims, such as a 25-yard sprint, and for the beginning and perhaps the finish of longer races.

Our second line of defense against ATP depletion in muscle is the system that is sometimes called the lactic acid energy system. This system is illustrated by the tank in the middle of the diagram, which has an intermediate-size tank and faucet. In this energy system, the fuel is stored muscle glycogen, which is simply a series of glucose molecules chemically bound together. When muscle ATP stores decline during intense exercise, the energy-producing process of glycolysis (the breakdown of sugar) is activated (the faucet is opened). Unlike the creatine phosphate system, this process is a sequence of reactions, each catalyzed by a different enzyme. Because of the increased number of reactions, this system has a slower maximum rate (smaller faucet) than the creatine phosphate system. The final products of glycolysis include ATP, of course, but also lactic acid.

The advantage of this energy system over the creatine phosphate system is that in a normally fed individual, there is an abundance of glycogen stored in the muscle. Because of the large fuel reserve for this system, glycolysis can sustain all-out swimming for between 30 seconds and about 1 minute. However, even in events lasting less than 1 minute, maximum swimming speed cannot be maintained. This is not because the muscles are running out of fuel (glycogen) but because the accumulation of lactic acid in the muscle fibers causes a decrease in the cell pH, or an increase in degree of acidity. Lowered pH brought on by lactic acid accumulation in turn reduces the ability of glycolysis to process glycogen and reproduce ATP at a fast enough rate to support the muscle contractions. In addition, the reduced pH inhibits the contraction process of muscles by decreasing the ability of calcium to activate the contractile proteins of muscle. In terms of our diagram, if lactic acid is allowed to accumulate, it begins to close the faucet on the glycogen tank and also begins to close the faucet connected to the muscle-energy-use tank. Because of the limitation imposed by lactic acid accumulation, the larger fuel reserve than the creatine phosphate system, and the slower maximal rate of ATP resynthesis, this energy system is most active in swimming distances from 100 to 200 yards. It is also active in longer distances, but the rate at which lactic acid is produced is much lower because of the slower speeds used in the longer distances.

Like the creatine phosphate system, the lactic acid system relies on fuel stored directly within the working muscle fibers. However, unlike the rapid restoration of the creatine phosphate after exercise, muscle glycogen tanks take from 12 to 24 hours to be refilled, and the source of the glucose for the recovery of glycogen is dietary carbohydrate. Considering the production of lactic acid and the need for dietary carbohydrate, this energy system does not burn clean and cannot be thought of as an immediately renewable energy source.

The energy system with the greatest total capacity (amount of energy irrespective of time) to reproduce ATP is referred to as the aerobic system (largest tank, smallest faucet), which relies on the oxidation of carbohydrate, fat, and/or protein. Of the three energy systems that have been presented, this is the only one that requires oxygen to function. This is why this system is referred to as aerobic—meaning that the energy transfer from the fuel to ATP requires participation of oxygen. The other systems are referred to as anaerobic—meaning that they do not need oxygen to function. Unlike the anaerobic systems, aerobic metabolism depends not only on fuels stored in muscle but also on fuels transported from organs relatively far removed from muscle and also on transport of oxygen from the lungs to the working muscle fibers. Because of its dependence on transport systems, the aerobic system is not immediately available in very short-duration, high-intensity swims, and even when oxygen uptake and transport are at maximum, the rate of ATP production is far less than would be needed to sustain maximum swimming speed. In other words, when the ATP-use faucet is opened all the way, the faucet on the aerobic tank, even if completely opened, would only be capable of meeting a small fraction of the demand for ATP. This is why physiologists often refer to endurance exercise as submaximal exercise.

Although the aerobic system has a choice between three possible fuel sources, it is unlikely that aerobic metabolism would ever rely exclusively on only one of the fuels. Instead, a mixture of these fuels is combusted, and the relative proportions of these fuels in the combustion mixture is determined mostly by the nutritional status of the swimmer but also by the intensity of the submaximal exercise. If a swimmer consumes a high-fat diet, then muscle glycogen stores will be low, and this will force aerobic metabolism to rely on fat and protein as the primary fuels, because glycogen is synthesized only from dietary carbohydrate. If, on the other hand, the diet contains ample carbohydrate, muscle glycogen can be restored between practice sessions and muscles will be able to use this fuel repeatedly over several days of training.

EXERCISE PHYSIOLOGY CONCERNS IN SWIMMING

Competition

An athlete's energy stores must be fine-tuned to a certain distance (duration) to reach competitive excellence. Swims may last from fewer than 30 seconds to more than 20 minutes.

Swims Lasting Less Than 30 Seconds

A 25-yard sprint requires maximum effort. This is analogous to opening the faucet on the muscle ATP tank all the way. Unless one or more of the energy systems' faucets are also opened, the level of the ATP in the muscle will drop. It is obvious from the diagram that the aerobic system is not the appropriate energy system because of the delay created by reliance on transport and the small size of the faucet. Even if we were to fully open the faucet on the lactic acid system, the rate of ATP use would far exceed the rate of ATP resynthesis from glycolysis. Thus, the energy system most suited to this kind of swim is the creatine phosphate system, which has the best chance of being able to match the rate of ATP use with the rate of ATP resynthesis. In reality, all three energy systems are fully activated in a sprint, but the creatine phosphate system is the only one that can respond quickly enough to have a significant impact on keeping up with energy demand. (Figure 4.3 shows the approximate percentage of contribution of each energy system to various swimming durations.)

You can prescribe training to modify this energy system in your swimmers. Within about 6 weeks of starting sprint training, your swimmers can slightly increase the amount of fuel (creatine phosphate) stored in this tank. In addition, there is some evidence that the maximum rate (size of the faucet) is increased by sprint training. These adaptations should, therefore, increase the maximal speed of your swimmers and allow them to maintain maximum speed for a slightly longer time. Remember that the magnitude of adaptation in this energy system is small—the results of these adaptations may be measured in only 10ths of a second over 20- to 30-second races. It is also important to point out that exclusive aerobic or endurance (distance) training has been shown to *reduce* the amount of stored creatine phosphate and may account for the loss of speed experienced by many swimmers during periods of training involving a great deal of swimming. It may be that including some sprint training in your distance swimmers' daily training plan will help prevent this drop, but no research has been done to test this hypothesis.

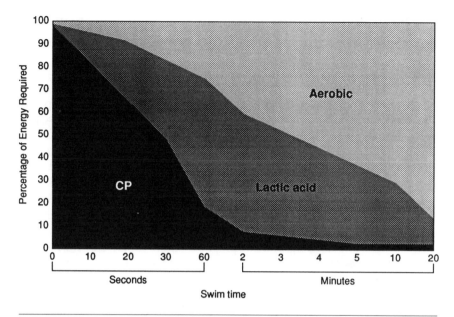

Figure 4.3 How energy systems work together at different all-out swimming durations to meet the energy need.

Swims Lasting 1 to 2 Minutes

A 100-yard competitive swim may last anywhere from a little over 40 seconds to slightly more than 1 minute, depending on the stroke and the swimmer's ability. Regardless of where in this range your swimmers fall, this is too long to expect the creatine phosphate system to play a major role in preventing muscle ATP depletion. Certainly, in the first 25 yards of the race, the creatine phosphate system will be the most significant energy system, but as the creatine phosphate tank runs down, the other energy systems play greater roles. The lactic acid system has less delay in response than the aerobic system and has a faster maximal rate of ATP resynthesis. Thus, this energy system becomes dominant during the final three quarters of the race. Consequently, muscle and blood levels of lactic acid are generally highest after races lasting about 2 minutes. The ability to maintain pace in the middle and end of these races is in large part determined by (a) how much lactic acid the swimmer accumulated for this pace, and (b) the swimmer's ability to physiologically and psychologically tolerate the lactic acid.

Modifications you can make to improve this energy system and thereby improve the performance of your middle-distance swimmers include

1. reducing their accumulation of lactic acid for a given pace,

2. increasing their physiological tolerance of accumulated lactic acid, and
3. increasing their psychological tolerance of accumulated lactic acid.

You can achieve the first goal by prescribing training to improve aerobic power (i.e., endurance training) and economy of swimming. Improving aerobic power helps minimize lactic acid accumulation by decreasing the response time of the aerobic system so it can play a slightly greater role in meeting the ATP demand of a given pace, while improving economy (decreased energy demand for given speeds) slows the rate of ATP use, allowing the aerobic system to play a greater role in the ATP supply.

You can reach the second goal by prescribing training to improve the buffer capacity of muscle (also known as the ability of muscle to minimize the pH disturbance caused by lactic acid). Proteins, bicarbonate, and creatine (not creatine phosphate) all act as buffers in muscle and reduce the pH drop associated with any given level of lactic acid accumulation. Another advantage of using the creatine phosphate energy ahead of the lactic acid system is that breakdown of creatine phosphate increases the buffer capacity of the muscles and can be thought of as a preparation for the upcoming accumulation of acid. Studies have shown that the ability of muscle to buffer lactic acid is improved by at least 6 weeks of intense training involving work bouts lasting 30 seconds to 1 minute with 4 to 8 minutes' rest between each. Endurance training has been shown to have no effect, either positive or negative, on muscle buffer capacity.

You can attain the final goal, of increasing pain tolerance, by improving the swimmer's motivation. For a discussion of such psychological factors, see chapter 2.

Swims Lasting 4 to 6 Minutes

Swims lasting 4 to 6 minutes include the 400-meter freestyle and individual medley, 400-yard individual medley, and 500-yard freestyle. This competitive distance is longer than the distance that could be supported by the creatine phosphate system or maximum activation of the lactic acid system, and yet the required pace is greater than the maximum rate of the aerobic system. Because of this, the lactic acid system and the aerobic system contribute nearly equally to resynthesizing ATP at the proper rate. The trick to optimizing performance in this distance is for your swimmers to select a pace that will result in lactic acid accumulation at a rate such that maximum lactate tolerance is reached right at the end of the race but not sooner. If the swimmer reaches maximum lactate tolerance before finishing the race, the obvious result is that muscular fatigue will cause the pace to slow. If the swimmer underestimates this pace, maximum lactate tolerance will not be reached, and the swimmer will have "too much left" and could have swum faster through the middle of the race.

This distance is also commonly used as a training distance in practices for improving the endurance capacity or aerobic capabilities of swimmers. In this case, however, the swimmers perform this distance at submaximal speeds. Thus, the swimmer can perform up to 8 to 12 repeats of this distance without experiencing excessive muscular fatigue. If the speed is slow enough, little, if any, lactic acid is accumulated. This is because the bulk of the ATP needs are met by the aerobic system, and the slow rate of the lactic acid system can be matched by the rate of lactic acid removal (a primarily aerobic process). This does not mean that the lactic acid system is not being used, only that its relatively slow rate is balanced by the rate of aerobic removal of lactic acid. If the pace is progressively increased on successive 400-yard repeats, a pace is eventually reached at which the rate of lactate production can no longer be matched by lactate removal. At this pace, lactate begins to accumulate, and muscular fatigue occurs within a few seconds or a couple of minutes, depending on how far the swimmer has exceeded this critical pace. The speed at which lactate can no longer be maintained at a steady level is called "maximum steady state," "anaerobic threshold," "lactate threshold," "onset of blood lactate accumulation," and other, less often used terms. The pace at maximum steady state has received much attention in recent years because it has been shown to be an excellent predictor of endurance performance potential and is perhaps a nearly ideal pace at which to train for improved endurance capacity. More will be said about this concept later in the chapter when training considerations are discussed.

Swims Lasting 10 to 20 Minutes

Distances ranging from 800 yards up to 1,650 yards are considered the distance events in competitive swimming, yet the time spent in these swims is considerably less than distance events in other sports, such as distance running, cycling, and cross-country skiing, that we consider endurance events. Nevertheless, in competitive swimming, our distance events are the aerobic endurance events, and good performance requires a great deal of participation from the aerobic system. The energetic difference between our shorter events and those of longer sporting events is that the pace used in a competitive event lasting 8 to 20 minutes is greater than the maximum steady-state pace discussed earlier. Thus, these events are not exclusively aerobic but rather require some additional energetic support from the lactic acid energy system. Again, finding the fastest possible pace that can be maintained for the distance without exceeding maximal lactate tolerance will result in the fastest time.

Warm-Up

The physiological demands of the races that were discussed in the previous section are probably affected to some extent by whether or not the swimmer has performed an adequate warm-up before the competition. The physiological purpose of warm-up is to elevate muscle temperature by increasing blood flow through the appropriate muscle groups. Presumably, if muscle temperature is increased, the adjustment time of the aerobic energy system will be decreased when the race is begun. This could, in turn, increase the aerobic contribution of any given swimming speed and thus decrease the accumulation of lactic acid. The possible positive impact on performance from this is obvious. Most of the research that has been done on the effects of warm-up supports this hypothesis as long as the timing of the precompetition warm-up is not too soon before the competition. It seems that the physiological effects of warm-up are lost within 15 to 20 minutes after the warm-up, and no reduction of lactic acid formation can be expected with longer delays. This should not be taken as a recommendation to skip warm-up if it precedes the competition by more than 20 minutes. One must remember that only one of the benefits of warm-up is physiological and there is still value in familiarizing swimmers with the physical environment in which they are expected to compete. All coaches can think of instances in which the pool's backstroke flags were placed at a distance that their swimmers weren't used to and swimmers who did not have a chance to familiarize themselves with them repeatedly missed their turns.

If the delay between warm-up and competition is greater than 20 minutes, and access to the water for prerace warm-ups is restricted, you can have your swimmers do some prerace stretching exercises on the deck. For stretching exercises, whether in place of a water warm-up or as a supplement to the water warm-up, the muscles should be warm before starting the stretching. To accomplish this, you can have your swimmers do about 5 to 10 minutes of light calisthenics before the stretching. There is no guarantee that stretching in place of a water warm-up can provide the same or even a similar effect as an in-water warm-up, but if it is the only alternative, you should use it.

Coaches and swimmers often ask what is the optimum pace or speed at which to warm up. There is no one answer to that question, but it seems that accumulation of lactic acid should be avoided and that any fast swimming should be followed by about 5 to 10 minutes of very slow swimming to help remove any lactate that may have accumulated.

Recovery From Races (Cool-Down)

Repeated competition during the day can result in feelings of residual fatigue that can negatively affect later races. It is therefore important that swimmers completely recover after each swim. Accumulated lactate must be removed, creatine phosphate must be restored, muscle pH must be rebalanced, metabolic products should be removed, body temperature should be normalized, and hormone responses to the swim should be reset to resting levels. All of these processes have different time courses for recovery, and some may take as long as an hour or more if the swimmer is allowed to engage in passive recovery (lying down or sitting). If, on the other hand, a 5- to 10-minute cool-down period of mild exercise is used, these recovery processes are accelerated.

Daily Training

The physiological requirements of competitive swimmers' daily training are exceptionally high. One of the great puzzles of physiology is why, if they compete in events that mostly last between 1 and 2 minutes, do swimmers train so much? Indeed it is true that swimmers often swim more miles per day than many marathoners run! The high training volumes of marathon runners can be justified by the fact that they are preparing to compete in an event that lasts over 2 hours. However, in recent years, many marathon runners have decreased their total training volume and added some faster interval training to help maintain their speed and reduce their risk of overuse injuries. Some swimming programs have also begun to experiment with reduced training volume in an effort to reduce the incidence of overtraining. Part of the reason swimming coaches feel the need to use so much training may be the fact that swimming races require great energy contributions from all three energy systems. Thus, some training aimed at each of the energy systems is necessary. Furthermore, the ability to tolerate the amount of work required to train all three energy systems requires remarkable recuperative powers. Because the recovery process seems to be accelerated in endurance-trained individuals, large volumes of aerobic training may be needed just to help recover from the anaerobic training.

PUTTING EXERCISE PHYSIOLOGY TO WORK FOR YOU

Your understanding of physiological principles can help you make decisions concerning the amount of training, the amount of rest needed by swimmers, and the intensity of training. Consideration must be given to training the energy systems that will most influence the performance of given events. This consideration of using the appropriate energy systems and targeting the training at developing the proper balance of the energy systems is known as the principle of *specificity of training*. Simply stated, the specificity principle means that the effects of training are not generalized over the whole body or to all energy systems. Rather, the effects of training appear to be localized within the trained muscle, and there seems to be very little carryover of improvement from one energy system to the next if only one form of training is used. An excellent example of this is the reduction of creatine phosphate stores that is caused by exclusive aerobic training. To use the specificity principle to your advantage, start planning the training by asking yourself what are the physiological requirements of the events the swimmer is training for. Once the components of this performance are identified, training strategies designed to target these components can be devised.

Training for Speed or Sprint Ability

Maximum speed has been repeatedly shown to correlate most closely to maximum propulsive power, the application of maximum power, and the ability to maintain maximum power for as long as 20 seconds or so. Likewise, the ability to regenerate ATP through the creatine phosphate system is an extremely important consideration in determining the ability to generate and maintain this power throughout the race. So, dry-land strength training is often an integral part of the sprint swimmers' daily training. Dry-land strength training should focus on developing the amount of strength required to generate as much propulsive power as possible without increasing muscle mass so much that water resistance becomes counterproductive. Research suggests that the type of strength training best for improving sprint performance is as specific to swimming as possible. From this standpoint, it may make sense to recommend that arm movements used in the strength exercise duplicate the swimming arm movements as much as possible. This way, you can be reasonably sure that the muscles that are trained are the muscles that will actually be used during the swimming event. However, many coaches like to use strength training exercises that isolate the muscle groups used in swimming. Isolated muscle exercises include triceps extension, lat pulls, biceps curls, and knee extension. There can be no doubt that this approach is effective in increasing the strength of these muscle groups. However, whether these improvements in strength result in improved swimming performance is not presently known. Some research shows no or very little correlation between strength of isolated muscle groups and performance of those muscle groups when performing the integrated movement. It may be that the better approach would be to conduct the power training program in the water with swimming as the mode of strength exercise. One way to accomplish this is to use some kind of tethered swimming device in which the swimmer is tied to a resisting device and attempts to swim away from the resistance. Although the mechanics of swimming with and without added resistance are certainly not the same, this may be the best of all possible ways to assure as much specificity of the strength training as possible (see Coaches' Clinic 4.2).

Eric's experience demonstrates that strength, although important to sprinters, may not improve performance unless it transfers to the movements actually used in competition. By adding tethered swimming to his strength regimen, Eric applied a very specific form of resistance training

---

COACHES' CLINIC 4.2: SHOWING SWIMMERS THE ROPES

Subject: Eric

Event: Sprint freestyle

Best time: 22.8 seconds for 50 yards

Goal time: 22.3 seconds

Discussion: Eric has excellent mechanics for streamlining off turns and starts, but his upper body strength seems low. He has been doing a variety of upper body strength exercises using free weights with heavy loads. Strength has improved in the weight room but has not yet improved his 50-yard performance.

Strategy: Two days per week Eric performs 10 sets of 10-yard swims while tethered by a rope attached to his waist and fed through pulleys to a bucket that hangs over the deck. When he swims out from the wall, the rope pulls the bucket off the deck. The weight in the bucket should be light at first but increased progressively over the next few weeks. This helps Eric to build strength and power as well as learn to apply the added strength to extra propulsion while swimming.

Result: More explosive power allows Eric to attain top speed earlier in the 50-yard race, resulting in a 0.5-second improvement.

to his development. Whether tethered swimming can negatively affect the stroke mechanics used in free swimming is a legitimate concern of some coaches. Currently there is no evidence that the altered mechanics used during the relatively infrequent tethered swimming carry over to free swimming.

Aside from strength training, swimmers generally perform repeated sprints of 25-yard, 50-yard, and half-length sprints. A typical sprint-training set may include 10 × 25 yard sprints on an interval that allows about 30 seconds' rest between each. This is fine, but you cannot expect your swimmers to be able to maintain their true sprint speeds for all 10 of these repeats, because the rest duration is too short to allow complete restoration of muscular creatine phosphate. Because creatine phosphate restoration takes between 1.5 and 3 minutes, sprint training within an interval set should allow long rest periods. If inadequate rest is allowed, the creatine phosphate energy may become quickly exhausted, forcing the swimmer to rely more on the lactic acid system during the second half of the training set. Once the dominant energy system is changed, the nature of the adaptation changes, and the swimmer might not get the desired effect of the sprint set. A general rule is that during sprinting, enough rest should be allowed to assure complete or near-complete recovery and to assure that the swimmer can reach peak velocities on each repeat.

Training for Middle-Distance Events

Middle-distance events in swimming consist of the 200- to 500-yard distances. A case could also be made for including the 100-yard distance in this classification, because although many coaches treat the 100-yard distance as a sprint, peak velocity cannot be maintained for more than a few seconds. Thus, the swimmer specializing in the 100-yard distance should be trained both as a sprinter and as a middle-distance swimmer.

Referring back to the model of energy use presented earlier in this chapter, you can see that events in this middle-distance range require elements of speed, lactate tolerance, and aerobic endurance. For these athletes, adequate speed or maximum velocity is essential to achieving their best possible performance. Let's use the example of a swimmer who has a best time of 2 minutes for a 200-yard event (see Coaches' Clinic 4.3).

Megan's example demonstrates that developing endurance in middle-distance swimmers is important from the standpoint that this allows them to swim closer to their maximum speed without reaching maximum lactate tolerance. The excellent background of aerobic training developed this in Megan. However, swimmers eventually get to a level where they swim so close to maximum speed that no further improvement can be

COACHES' CLINIC 4.3: A MATTER OF TOLERANCE

Subject: Megan

Event: Middle-distance

Present best time: 2:00 in 200 yards

Best 50 time: 27.0 seconds

Goal time: 1:58 in 200 yards

Discussion: Megan has done a great deal of aerobic training. The pacing strategy she uses is 28 seconds on the first 50 and 30.5 seconds on the next three 50s. This pacing is nearly ideal and represents "even" pacing (the first 50 is faster mostly because of the advantage offered by the dive).

Recent performance: Megan was asked to swim the first 50 yards at a faster pace than usual and try to "hang on." This involved a near-sprint effort, but her middle 50s dropped off to 32 seconds. Her final 200 time was 2:01.

Strategy: Megan would benefit more from improving her maximum speed so that a 27-second first 50 does not require a full sprint. The muscles would *ease open* the faucet on the lactic acid energy system, resulting in less lactate accumulation early in the race. She could then maintain faster 50 splits in the middle of the race.

Prescription: Lactate tolerance: 6 × 100, with 3 minutes rest
Lactate tolerance/speed: 8 × 50, with 3 minutes rest
Speed: 8 × 25, with 2 minutes' rest
Two lactate-tolerance sets per week
Two speed sets per week

Results: After 5 weeks, Megan's 200 time dropped 2 seconds.

expected without raising the ceiling set by the maximum speed. This is analogous to designing a race car with a top speed of 100 miles per hour that can run all day at 95 miles per hour. This car would never win a race against another car that can only maintain 60% of top speed but has a top speed of 200 miles per hour. Obviously, the ideal machine has an extremely high top speed and the endurance capacity to maintain long-duration efforts at levels as near as possible to top speed.

The approach that helped Megan reach her goal time was to increase maximal speed and lactate tolerance while maintaining excellent endurance. Thus, it should be clear that training for the middle distance is best designed to include speed, lactate tolerance, and aerobic endurance. A training program that focuses on only one or two of these elements will result in improved performance, but not as much improvement as we would expect from the combined effect of all three forms of training.

Training for Distance Events

The distance events include the 800-meter to 1,650-yard events, and the requirements of these events are conceptually similar to those of middle-distance events. Speed, lactate tolerance, and aerobic endurance contribute to performance, but they make different relative contributions here than in middle-distance events. As the distance of the swim increases, speed is relegated to a progressively more minor role and aerobic endurance becomes increasingly more important. Although there is no research at present that has examined the importance of lactate tolerance to performance of these distance events, it is reasonable to expect that because the distance events are swum at paces faster than anaerobic threshold, a high tolerance of lactic acid would aid performance, especially in the latter part of the race.

If the importance of both aerobic endurance and lactate tolerance in distance events is accepted, then we are faced with somewhat of a paradox with regard to training. Obviously, these swimmers should participate in some forms of training designed to increase lactic acid accumulation and other forms of training specifically to decrease the amount of lactate accumulated at the race speed. At first glance, these two adaptations seem to be opposite, and one might think they would counteract each other. However, these adaptations probably are compatible and may be best understood using the analogy of an economy car with a turbo-booster attached. As long as the speed requirement is low, the car's engine will burn fuel at a slow rate, but when needed, the turbo can be activated for short high-energy bursts to produce higher speeds. In the swimmer this may translate to an ability to swim as close as possible to race pace without accumulating lactate but being able to generate and tolerate fairly fast rates of lactate accumulation as the race strategy demands (see Coaches' Clinic 4.4).

Constructing the Single Training Session

The adaptations that take place in muscle and the other organ systems are in response to physical stress that exceeds that normally encountered.

COACHES' CLINIC 4.4: GO THE DISTANCE

Subject:	David
Event:	Distance
Present best time:	17:20 in 1,650 4:52 in 500
Goal time:	17:00 in 1,650
Discussion:	David's practices have included 3-4 lactate-tolerance sets per week for the last several weeks. These have helped him develop excellent short-term lactate tolerance as shown by his excellent 500 time. However, his 500 splits in the 1650 were 5:05, 5:17, and 5:22 on the way to a 17:20. This indicates that, even at 5:05, he is swimming too far above his lactate threshold, and this is the likely cause of the excessive fatigue later in the race.
Strategy:	David should probably attempt to increase his lactate threshold to a faster speed so that he can swim closer to his best 500 time during the 1,650. In addition, 3-4 lactate tolerance sets per week is excessive and may cause an overtrained state.

COACHES' CLINIC 4.4: CONTINUED

Prescription: Decrease lactate tolerance work to no more than 2 sets per week and replace with threshold work such as 20 × 100 with 15 seconds' rest averaging about 1:04 at first and gradually decreasing the average time to about 1:01 over the next several weeks. This may be alternated with longer distance work such as 3 × 800 with 20 seconds' rest, concentrating on even pacing.

Results: The combined effect of resting from so much lactate-tolerance work and increasing the long, slow distance work improved David's ability to swim closer to his best 500 pace without suffering as much fatigue. In the next meet, David swam the first 500 yards in 5:06, followed by a 5:09, and a 5:11 with a final time in the 1,650 of 16:58.

Each individual work period contributes to the total accumulated physical stress that, within certain limits, creates a physiological environment inducing adaptation. This is referred to as the *overload* principle and is one of the key concepts in designing swimming training. Overzealous application of the overload principle, however, seems to inhibit adaptation rather than promote it. Thus, one of the greatest mysteries of training prescription is how to provide the athlete with small but adequate doses of physical stress that will produce the desired effect with minimum risk of negative side effects. Designing training is therefore similar to physicians prescribing medicine: It involves mixing equal parts of science, intuition, trial-and-error experience, and consideration for individual responses.

Warm-Up

Every training session should begin with a warm-up period designed to physiologically and psychologically prepare the athlete for the subsequent training. Objectives to be accomplished during the warm-up period include elevated muscle temperature, increased flexibility, motivation to train correctly, and establishment of training goals for the session. Generally, these goals can be achieved within a time frame of about 10 to 20 minutes. Flexibility exercises appropriate for swimmers include but are not limited to the shoulder stretch, upper arm stretch, ankle stretch, calf stretch, and thigh stretch. Here are some general recommendations for stretching:

- Start with light calisthenics to prewarm the muscles and connective tissue.
- Stretch the muscle to the point of tension.
- Hold this position for 10 seconds.
- As tension diminishes, stretch a little farther.
- Hold the new position 10 seconds.
- Change to a new muscle and repeat.

The stretching period should then be followed by some warm-up swimming using slow swims at about 50% to 60% efforts. Many coaches prefer to have swimmers mix some kicking, pulling, and whole-stroke drills to warm up all the muscle groups to be used in the training. This is a very reasonable approach, and it helps to eliminate the boredom that may arise from always swimming exactly the same warm-up.

Sprint Training Sets

Sprint training sets consist of repeated swims in the half-length to 25-yard distance, with large amounts of rest between each swim. The purposes of these sets include raising the amount of stored creatine phosphate and the rate at which this extra fuel can be processed. In terms of performance benefits, sprint sets help to increase the swimmer's maximum velocity and slightly increase the amount of time that the maximum velocity can be sustained.

In addition to the general recommendations in Figure 4.4, give some consideration to the placement of sprint training sets in the training session. Coaches seem to get into the habit of placing sprint training sets at

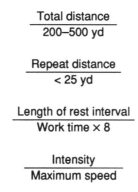

Total distance
200–500 yd

Repeat distance
< 25 yd

Length of rest interval
Work time × 8

Intensity
Maximum speed

Figure 4.4 General recommendations for sprint training sets.

the end of the practice. Because most swimmers seem to like to sprint, this is an effective way of ending a practice on a fun note. However, sprint sets should be placed early in the practice at least as often as they occur late in the practice. The reason for this is that if sprinting is always done at the end of practice, the fatigue from the earlier work sets may inhibit the swimmer's ability to truly sprint (i.e., achieve and maintain maximum velocity). If you occasionally place your sprint sets early in practice, your swimmers will be able to sprint while still in a somewhat rested state and perhaps perform better. The possible fatiguing effects the early-practice sprinting may have on later sets may, however, concern you. Fortunately, if the sprint training set is constructed properly (with near-complete recovery between swims and maximum duration of each swim less than 20 seconds), there should be very little residual fatigue to carry over into the rest of the practice. Figure 4.4 gives general recommendations for constructing sprint training sets.

Lactate-Tolerance Sets

To improve one's physiological tolerance of lactate accumulation requires repeated exposure to high concentrations of blood and muscle lactic acid. Needless to say, this type of training requires very intense efforts and is remarkably stressful, so lactate-tolerance sets are not generally recommended for more than about 2 or 3 training sessions per week and should probably not be used during the first 4 to 6 weeks of the season. Some general guidelines for constructing these sets appear in Figure 4.5.

Prescribing the appropriate intensity or pace for these swims is important. Unlike for sprint training, do not insist that the swimmers go all-out on each of the repeats. Because recovery is incomplete between swims, the all-out strategy would cause diminished performance during the second half of lactate-tolerance sets. A better approach to pacing

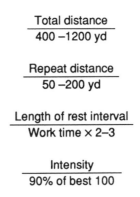

$$\frac{\text{Total distance}}{400-1200 \text{ yd}}$$

$$\frac{\text{Repeat distance}}{50-200 \text{ yd}}$$

$$\frac{\text{Length of rest interval}}{\text{Work time} \times 2-3}$$

$$\frac{\text{Intensity}}{90\% \text{ of best 100}}$$

Figure 4.5   General recommendations for lactate-tolerance sets.

with these sets is to try for the fastest possible average pace within the constraints offered by the number of repeats and the length of the rest intervals. Some have recommended that paces equivalent to roughly 85% to 95% of best 100-yard swim be used in lactate-tolerance sets. This is a wide range, though, and it is most useful as an initial guess for determining the proper pace.

Another consideration for lactate-tolerance sets concerns the type of recovery that should be used between each of the swims. The choices are passive or active recovery. Passive recovery involves floating, sitting, or lying down between the swims. Active recovery consists of fairly easy swimming during the rest intervals. Of the two methods, active recovery is the better recovery method for lactate-tolerance sets. Easy swimming at paces less than about 60% of best 100 pace are suitable and will help speed up the clearance of lactate and restore the pH balance within the muscles. This helps to insure that the swimmers are able to maintain their paces over the whole set and causes the muscles to repeatedly activate glycolysis. This repeated production of lactate and the associated repeated fall in muscular pH are very likely the triggers for the adaptations that facilitate lactate tolerance. Therefore, let the swimmer's ability to maintain a constant pace dictate whether the length and type of recovery interval is adequate.

Aerobic Conditioning Sets

Training bouts specifically designed to improve the aerobic energy system in muscle and the cardiorespiratory system are historically an integral part of the competitive swimmer's daily training (see Figure 4.6 for general

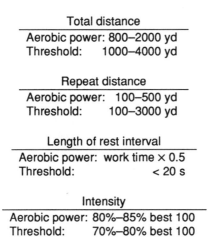

Total distance	
Aerobic power:	800–2000 yd
Threshold:	1000–4000 yd

Repeat distance	
Aerobic power:	100–500 yd
Threshold:	100–3000 yd

Length of rest interval	
Aerobic power:	work time × 0.5
Threshold:	< 20 s

Intensity	
Aerobic power:	80%–85% best 100
Threshold:	70%–80% best 100

Figure 4.6 General recommendations for aerobic sets.

recommendations). This is perhaps most evident in the first several weeks of the season, when coaches rely heavily on aerobic training to develop their swimmers' endurance base. Once this first phase of the season is passed, the proportion of aerobic training is generally decreased somewhat to make room for more race-specific forms of training, such as sprinting and lactate-tolerance training.

Even in these later stages of the season, the total volume of aerobic endurance training exceeds the volume of other forms of training. This is consistent with research observations indicating that maximum oxygen uptake (the most widely used test of maximal aerobic power) shows very little, if any, increase after 6 to 8 weeks of aerobic training. Although continued use of aerobic conditioning throughout the season may not further enhance the maximal aerobic power, it may serve other purposes. For example, some researchers claim that although maximal oxygen uptake does not continue to rise with continued training, the speed or pace at the anaerobic threshold will continue to improve. In other words, the athlete first raises the aerobic ceiling set by $\dot{V}O_2max$, then develops an ability to work as near as possible to the $\dot{V}O_2max$ without accumulating lactate. The longer and slower swimming done in aerobic sets may also be responsible in part for helping swimmers develop economical stroke patterns. If this is true, the benefit would lie in the fact that improved economy would mean less energy use at the same speed.

Finding the Ideal Pace

Prescribing the ideal pace at which to train for optimum improvements in aerobic conditioning is difficult, and this pace is not the same for each swimmer. This is why the same prescription cannot be effectively used for a whole team (e.g., everybody maintain 32 seconds per 50 yards). The next sections describe several methods for prescribing an aerobic training pace.

Self-Selected Pacing.   Allowing swimmers to select their own training paces for the aerobic sets is also less than optimal; it has been shown that when self-selected paces are used, roughly one third of the swimmers will exercise at too low an intensity, one third will be close to an appropriate intensity, and one third will overwork. If you are satisfied with a 33% success rate, and as long as one third of the team happens to belong to the middle group, this prescription method is fine. It's more likely, though, that in any given year a team will not be evenly represented by these groups. Thus, in some years there may be more swimmers in the first group, prompting you to reflect at the end of the season about how difficult it was to motivate the team to train. In another year, there may be a disproportionate number of swimmers from the third group, getting you excited about how great a team this will be, only to have your hopes tempered in the middle of the season by the extraordinary number of swimmers who get overtrained and do not compete up to expectations. Then sometimes purely by chance, the majority of the swimmers on a team come from the middle group, everything in the training seems to work well, and the season culminates with remarkable improvements exceeding even your expectations.

Using a prescription technique more objective than self-selected paces will not guarantee that all swimmers on a team will have a magical season, but it improves the odds of it and may result in more consistent success in the training program. In an effort to individualize the aerobic training prescription, sport scientists have devised several methods that are at least somewhat sensitive to individual differences in working capacity.

Heart Rate Prescriptions.   Perhaps the most widely used methods are based on the exercise heart rate. One of the greatest drawbacks of heart rate prescriptions, however, is that exercise at a given heart rate may be below anaerobic threshold for some and above threshold for others. This variability is related in part to the fact that individuals with greater endurance abilities generally can exercise at higher heart rates before reaching anaerobic threshold. Determining the heart rate at the lactate-accumulation threshold for each individual may eliminate this problem. Unfortunately, however, as a swimmer improves in aerobic conditioning, heart rate at the threshold pace increases. Without frequent retesting of the heart rate at threshold, you would not know which new heart rate to use in the prescription. The heart rate method that perhaps does the best job of accounting for changes in the relationship between heart rate and lactate threshold is described in Figure 4.7.

Percentage of Best Time.   Others prefer to use training paces equivalent to certain percentages of the swimmer's best competition time. This method is also plagued by the fact that increased aerobic conditioning is associated with higher percentages of best time before lactate threshold is reached. Thus, recommendations that come from studies on a given population of swimmers are only applicable to that part of the swimming population used in the study and in that particular phase of training.

Blood Lactate Measurements.   Becoming dissatisfied with the lack of precision in these prescription methods, some coaches and sport scientists have experimented with prescribing the aerobic training intensity based on blood lactate levels. Simply put, this method requires first a testing session in which the swimmers swim a series of 200- to 400-yard swims at progressively faster paces until the final swim is nearly all-out. After each of the swims, a small sample of blood is collected from a fingertip or earlobe, and each sample is analyzed later for lactate concentration. The range in swimming pace that most closely corresponds to a

Week	% Heart rate reserve (HRR)
0	65
4	70
8	75
12	80
16	85

Sample Calculation

HR max*	200
− HR rest	− 50
HRR	150
× %	× 0.70
	105
+ HR rest	+ 50
THR	155

Figure 4.7 Appropriate target heart rates (THR) through the season—used for prescribing aerobic training.
*HRmax can be estimated by measuring HR immediately after a 4 to 5 minute time-trial performance.

blood lactate concentration between 2 and 4 millimoles per liter (mM) is then used as the aerobic training pace range. Of course, as the swimmer's aerobic conditioning improves or as economy improves, the speed at which 2 to 4 mM of blood lactate is reached changes. Frequent testing to reevaluate the aerobic training pace is therefore required, especially in the early part of the season when these factors change rather quickly. Nutritional status can also affect this method, because a low-carbohydrate intake during training can reduce muscle glycogen stores. Because the fuel for the lactic acid energy system is glycogen, testing athletes in a glycogen-depleted state may underestimate the blood lactate response to given speeds. This may lead to the erroneous conclusion that the athlete has experienced an improvement in conditioning requiring a faster pace prescription. As discussed early in this chapter, chronic glycogen depletion can occur after several consecutive days of heavy training combined with inadequate carbohydrate intake. Ironically, then, if you relied on blood lactate as the sole means of prescribing training, you could make the mistake of giving this swimmer a *faster pace prescription*, when what the athlete really needs is a few recovery days of less intensive swimming!

Planning the Season

Like your swimmers, you also need recovery periods, so don't start to plan for next season the day after the championships. You should start some elements of planning, however, while the prior season is still fresh in your mind. In particular, this is an excellent time to make a few notes about the season that should be taken into consideration when next season's planning begins in earnest.

Each season should be thought of as consisting of three major phases, including an early-season phase, a midseason competitive phase, and the championship phase. The first phase lasts about 6 to 8 weeks and may, because of short high school seasons, stretch well into the competitions. This phase should consist of progressive development of aerobic conditioning and strength with *gradual* addition of sprint swimming and lactate-tolerance training. The second phase may last 4 to 8 weeks, depending on the total season length. Training content in this phase is centered around developing specific adaptations required by the different strokes and distances. Consequently, this is the part of the season where sprint training and lactate-tolerance training become a focus. Aerobic conditioning drills should still be used for maintaining prior adaptations and continued development of economy. The championship phase occurs during the last 2 to 8 weeks of the season, again depending on the season length and the number of championship meets in which the swimmers compete. This phase can also be referred to as the taper phase, because this is the time to gradually reduce the training load, bringing the swimmer to peak performance potential.

Some coaches are now experimenting with dividing the season into 4- to 6-week blocks referred to as mesocycles. Each mesocycle is thought of and planned almost as a miniseason, starting with gradual progression, switching to specific conditioning, and ending in the last week with a period of reduced work that acts like a minitaper. Ideally, these mesocycles should be planned so that a high-priority meet follows the final week of the cycle. The next mesocycle starts again with progression, but the training load is equivalent to roughly the middle of the previous cycle. The season is therefore a series of mesocycles connected in such a way that progression throughout the season is analogous to taking three steps forward, one step back, three steps forward, one back, and so on. The proposed benefits of this strategy are better competitive performances throughout the season and less risk of overtraining, without sacrificing the amount of overall improvement in the season.

KEYS TO SUCCESS

- **Consider the energy systems that support each swimming event when designing the training program.**
- **Target the main training bouts directly at the specific physiological adaptations desired.**

- Each energy system is limited by the amount of fuel available to the muscle during exercise.

- General physiological principles hold true for all swimmers, but each swimmer has individual characteristics that must be considered in planning and modifying the training.

- Progressive application of physical stress with adequate recovery is paramount among factors determining the amount of adaptation swimmers will experience.

- The correct race-pace strategy should be planned with considerations of the competition and energy requirements of the event.

CHAPTER 5

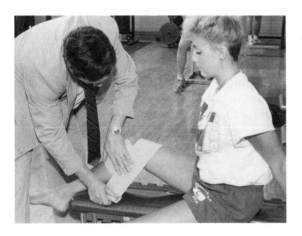

Sports Medicine: Managing Injuries

Bruce McAllister
North Central College

Al used to have one of the best breaststrokes on the team. Today he's on the deck icing his knee. He won't be swimming today. He has too little strength and too much pain while doing the breaststroke.

Bill is over in the corner wearing his sweats. He has a cotton wick in his ear because of an ear infection that has eliminated him from today's competition.

Sally is sitting with an icepack on her ankle. She had a problem pushing off from the wall a couple of months ago. It seems to have worsened, so she won't be able to swim in today's meet.

How many times have you come to the pool deck and noticed an athlete icing a months-old injury—an injury that icing and rest should already have healed? The previous scenarios are a daily occurrence in the sport of swimming, while other sports (e.g., football, basketball, and soccer) have recognized the value of having an athletic trainer. Is it possible that some swimming injuries could be prevented? Is it possible that those athletes who are now idly watching their teammates compete could have been helping their team complete a winning season, if an athletic trainer had been available? Also, would they have reached the goals that they had set for themselves? In many cases, the answer is yes!

WHY SPORTS MEDICINE IS IMPORTANT

The high schools, colleges, and universities are not monetarily or logistically at fault for the fact that sports medicine has not been a prominent force in the sport of swimming. The major problem is the fact that there are not enough personnel to assume that role. Because of this, coaches of age-group, interscholastic, and intercollegiate swimming have been burdened by sports medicine problems of which they were unaware and for which they have not been trained. This is more evident in swimming than in other sports.

Proper preventive treatment and rehabilitation techniques can help you and your swimmers attain your goals. The key is prevention. Just as the football player is taped, the swimmer can be massaged. Just as the soccer player is protected with shin guards, the swimmer can be consulted and directed toward a course of injury prevention. Just as the basketball player goes through a program of flexibility and psychological and physiological training, so can the swimmer. Unfortunately, in the absence of a sports medicine professional, this responsibility is added to the role of the coach, who often does not have the resources or backing to carry out all of the goals of the "major" sports. The objective of this chapter is to help you understand the role of sports medicine in injury prevention, treatment, and rehabilitation and its contribution to your swimmers' well-being.

Many new sports medicine techniques are in the forefront for swimming, but swimmers need to stay in close contact with a physician who is readily available and familiar with aquatic sports. Athletic trainers are learning new techniques developed especially for swimmers. These techniques have been tested through research studies and are detailed in literature devoted to the care of swimmers.

Swimming is both a recreational and competitive sport, and it remains the most popular participatory sport in the United States today. Swimming is excellent for achieving physical fitness and for rehabilitating injuries.

From a competitive standpoint, swimming requires a dedication to practice, concentration, and physical exertion that is not required for other athletic abilities and activities. Minute differences in stroke, breathing, or attitude may make the difference between the top swimmer and the opponent.

Sports medicine is a multidisciplinary approach, one of many modalities in coaching that, when used properly, can help individuals reach their potential. If you follow the prevention, treatment, and rehabilitation techniques described in this chapter, and work closely with your team physician or trainer, your swimmers will be in the water participating and not sidelined with injuries.

The Sports Medicine Team

A sports medicine "team" should consist of specialists in many different areas, with you, as coach, acting as maestro and bringing in as many talents as necessary to help your team. A number of people in the community are usually willing to be involved, many of whom offer their services voluntarily for the sake of supporting local athletes. It is important that all individuals involved in your program be united by a strong interest in swimming, diving, and aquatics in general. The people you choose to assist in your program must be familiar with your goals and those of the athletes and have some experience in working with swimmers.

Picture your sports medicine team as a large wheel (see Figure 5.1), with yourself as the hub. This team may include a certified athletic trainer, a family physician, an orthopedist, an ear-nose-throat physician, a physical therapist, a registered nurse, a massage therapist, a paramedic, a sport psychologist, a podiatrist, a dentist, and a dermatologist. Many of the specialists in this wheel will be brought into play after the family physician has requested counsel for a particular athlete. These resource people are often willing to provide their services in exchange for admission to the sport events.

SPORTS MEDICINE CONCERNS IN SWIMMING

Concerns in swimming are many and varied—from individual success to team success to the school's prestige and revenue coming in from meets. You and the athletic trainer are concerned primarily about overuse resulting from strenuous training and acute problems caused by sudden injury. It is imperative that you emphasize prevention of swimming injuries. With this in mind, we will first discuss overall preventive conditioning of the swimmer.

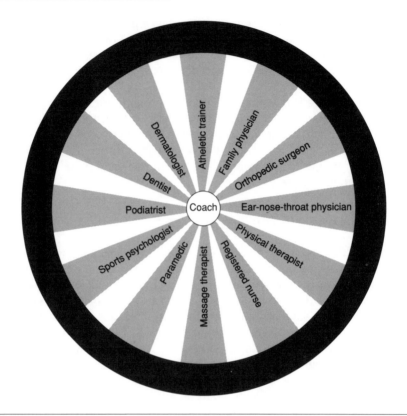

Figure 5.1 The sports medicine team wheel.

Overall Preventive Conditioning of the Swimmer

Prevention of injuries is best achieved by general fitness. Fitness has varied facets and encompasses psychological health as well as physiological factors such as flexibility and strength.

Psychological

You must be familiar with the psychological makeup of each swimmer. Because of the many different temperaments of athletes on a team, balancing rehabilitation programs, treatment routines, and different athletes' responses is difficult. You should talk to your swimmers about injury prevention at the onset of practice and let athletes with injuries know that they are expected to participate in practice—if they are not able to do full practices then suggest restricted practices, such as kicking at the side of the pool, riding a stationary bike, and so on. No one should be allowed to miss practice because of an injury. It is important to show concern for the athletes and to emphasize that through prevention they can help themselves become stronger, therefore better, and overcome many future psychological problems.

General Physiological

An athlete's physiological training (through strength, flexibility, and different tests of potential) is extremely important. There are many good texts and guides in the field of swimming that describe the physiological makeup of swimmers (and see chapter 4). Because swimmers are all different, they should be treated as individuals, even though this will not be easy if you have a big team.

Exercise physiologists from local colleges may help you understand some of the physiological problems that lead to sports injuries. Administration of physiological exams will prove beneficial. Body-fat calibration, height and weight measurement, and cardiovascular screening will all provide useful information for getting the most from your athletes. This also tends to create in the swimmers a keen awareness and interest regarding their bodies and overall health. The more swimmers know about their bodies and how they can be improved, the more improvement they will see. The local college often has master's degree students who are willing to conduct screening programs and collect data for use in their research program. Physiological data provide a very important ingredient to the total sports medicine picture (see chapter 4).

Flexibility.   Flexibility is extremely important for swimmers. Swimmers with poor flexibility will be especially vulnerable to injury if they undertrain and then go overboard during practice or competition. Injuries are also more likely for the swimmer who achieves a very flexible upper body but totally disregards the lower body. Stretching should be balanced with proper strength, and no stretch should be executed beyond the range of motion that the athlete will use in swimming. For example, you can always spot the swimmers who have incorrectly trained when you see them crossing their elbows behind them before competition. There is no stroke in swimming that requires such a movement. Many experts believe that exceeding this range of motion causes laxity in the joint, dislocation problems, compromised strength, and reduced stroke efficiency.

Flexibility exercises should be performed to help maintain fluid movement through the complete range of motion for a particular stroke. The athlete should feel fluid mobility throughout the range of motion while in the water. Flexibility exercises should be performed after an initial warm-up, which could take place in the pool (e.g., four to six slow laps). You might choose to have all your swimmers do the flexibility program as a group, so you can more easily supervise their movements.

An excellent upper body exercise is the anterior shoulder stretch (see Figure 5.2). This movement, which stretches the deltoid and front chest muscles (pectoralis, major and minor), should be slow and controlled, with the head moving toward the opposite shoulder as the hand is placed on the wall. The stretch is held for 25 seconds. It is beneficial for the breaststroke and the freestyle.

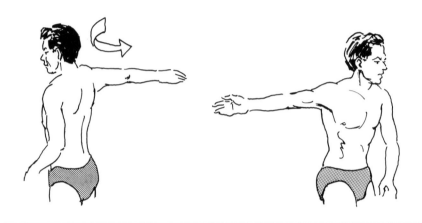

Figure 5.2 Anterior shoulder stretch using a wall for resistance.

The posterior shoulder stretch (see Figure 5.3) extends the posterior deltoid and latissimus dorsi and is useful for the breaststroke, freestyle, and especially the backstroke. Athletes lower in unison to their knees, putting their arms out in front and pulling back with straight arms. They will move out and in, stretching slowly and holding for 25 seconds. There should be a slight and even pull on the outside of the lateral aspect of the body.

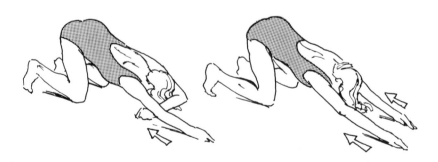

Figure 5.3 Posterior shoulder stretch for stretching the latissimus dorsi.

The over-the-head stretch is an excellent flexibility exercise that helps stretch the anterior, middle, and posterior deltoid, and the pectoralis major and minor, and incorporates the trapezius and latissimus dorsi (see Figure 5.4). The stretch is done with an even motion. The athletes start with their arms held out in front of them holding onto towels and moving their arms up over their heads. The first position, with arms stretched over the head, should be held for 20 seconds. In the second position, the arms are extended behind the athlete for 20 seconds, then are moved down the back to waist level and are held for 20 seconds. This is repeated four times to increase the amount of stretch. As athletes become more proficient, they may move their hands closer together on the towel. They should not be allowed to cross their elbows behind them.

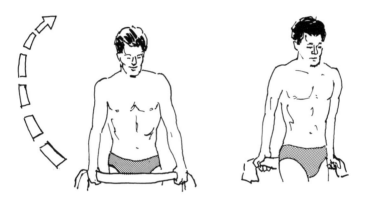

Figure 5.4   Over-the-head stretch for chest, shoulder, and upper back muscles.

Another stretch for the shoulder muscles incorporates the use of a bar (see Figure 5.5). With hands shoulder-width apart on the bar, the athletes bend their knees slightly and hold the stretch for 30 seconds. This provides a stretch to the trapezius, triceps, forearm extensors, and the latissimus dorsi. This stretch should be repeated four times.

Flexibility protocol for the lower body includes a quadricep stretch, which provides a beneficial stretch for the quadriceps, hamstrings, and the extensors in the foot and lower leg (see Figure 5.6). Note that the subject should not have the knee in front of the ankle but drops the hips to increase the stretch. This position should be held for each leg, and the stretch is repeated three times.

The ankle area is extremely important in swimming but often overlooked. An excellent ankle stretch is to kneel, then push forward with the thigh while lowering the heel, using a slow, controlled movement (see Figure 5.7). This movement, which is beneficial for all strokes, provides

Figure 5.5   Bar stretch for muscles of the arm and upper back.

Figure 5.6   Quadricep stretch for quadriceps, hamstrings, and extensor muscles of the foot and lower leg.

an excellent stretch for the latissimus dorsi and the quad on the bent knee. The position should be held for 20 seconds and repeated three times on each ankle.

The kneeling back stretch is done while sitting on the feet and then slowly moving forward until the head is near the ground (see Figure 5.8). This exercise extends the lower back and lumbar and is beneficial for all strokes. The hands are placed on the floor for balance. It is important that, if the athletes are very tight, they progress very slowly with this stretch.

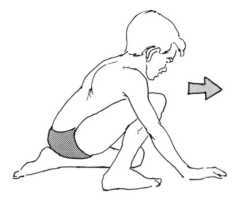

Figure 5.7   Ankle stretch that also benefits the latissimus dorsi and the quadriceps.

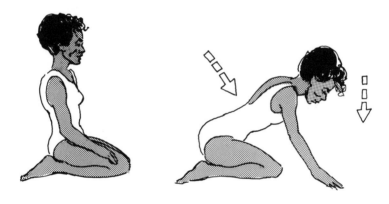

Figure 5.8   Kneeling back stretch for the lower back.

There should be no bouncing during the stretch, which should be held for approximately 20 seconds and repeated three times.

The lying neck stretch extends the cervical muscles and the latissimus dorsi (see Figure 5.9). The swimmers lie on their backs with knees up and pull their heads slowly forward with their hands, making sure their backs are not pulled off the floor. This position should be held for 10 seconds and repeated three times.

For the hip and groin area, the athletes should sit with the soles of their feet together and pulled up toward the groin area. The movement (see Figures 5.10, a and b) is from the hips (not the shoulders), bringing the feet up toward the buttocks and putting a mild, prolonged stretch on the adductor muscle. This exercise is excellent for breaststrokers, because it stretches the adductor muscle group that is often tight in swimmers after

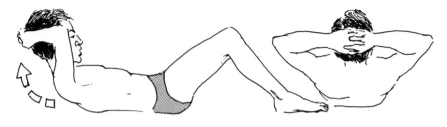

Figure 5.9   Cervical stretch for neck and latissimus dorsi.

Figure 5.10   Groin stretch.

practice or competition. The stretch should be held for 30 seconds, swimmers going into and coming out of the stretch slowly, and should be repeated three times.

You should constantly review the flexibility exercises and be aware of each individual's progress. Flexibility exercises, if done on a continual basis, will prevent many injuries during the season. Have your swimmers also do these exercises at home, especially when they rise in the morning. Parents may wish to be shown these exercises so they can be involved in their children's training program. Though flexibility exercises may be tedious at times, they can be made fun for a group and the rewards are great.

Strength.   Strength should be balanced with flexibility. Finding this balance in each individual is difficult and requires a thorough knowledge of the individual athlete's stroke.

The main problem with swimming is that there may be no real off-season. Most swimmers practice or are in meets during the summer and winter, so the season can be 12 months a year. Because of this, you will have to decide when to use high-rep/low-weight, low-rep/high-weight, freeweights, or isokinetics techniques. We know that a properly advised program, followed by a flexibility routine, can prevent serious injury from occurring later in the season.

Strengthening routines should concentrate not only on the chest and upper body, but also on the muscles in the lower leg. These include the adductor muscles (the muscles that bring the leg into the midline of the body) and the muscles on the outside of the leg that help stabilize and possibly prevent injury to the medial side of the knee. Strengthening the ankles through rotational exercises and calf raises is extremely important for the ankle and foot area. Include in your strengthening and flexibility programs the actual movements your swimmers will perform in the water. By mimicking the stroke and kick patterns in the flexibility and strength routines, the swimmers will reinforce what is expected of them in the water and also strengthen that stroke or kick through the proper range of motion.

Again, as for flexibility, supervise all strength programs and monitor the progress of each individual in writing. This will not only help prevent injury or movement that might hinder the athlete, but it will also provide you with valuable information during the training period. (See chapter 4.)

Bone, Tendon, and Ligament Injuries in Swimming

Coaches agree that swimmer's shoulder is the primary concern for the swimming team. Swimmer's shoulder (a very general term) has been researched heavily, and many treatments have been developed to eliminate the problem. For injuries that have been diagnosed by a physician as supraspinatus tendinitis or inflammation of the tendons within the shoulder joint itself, the following treatment can help prevent further spreading of the condition. It has been utilized at all levels and has proven to be very successful.

Swimmer's Shoulder

Evaluation. Swimmer's shoulder is a very frustrating problem for the coach. Often termed bursitis, tendinitis, inflammation, and so on, swimmer's shoulder is difficult to treat, and the outcome is unpredictable. Consultation with the sports medicine team, specifically the certified athletic trainer and orthopedic surgeon, will hopefully answer questions and identify appropriate treatments. Obviously, treatment would not be necessary if proper prevention had been instituted.

Tendinitis in a shoulder never happens overnight. It undoubtedly started many years before, probably during the early years of training for competitive swimming, as in the age-group or scholastic program. It has most likely been masked behind the "overuse syndrome" and has finally come into view. Physiologically, what occurs is that initially some tendon fibers are torn. With each ensuing contraction, the healing breach tears again, causing more pain and an inflamed scar.

In the case of muscle tissue, a strain causes some fibers to part. The body then lays down scar tissue to heal the area. This scar tissue glues the fibers, not only longitudinally but transversely. When the muscle contracts, the adhesions cause pain and further tearing.

With ligaments, the overuse or tearing can cause the scar tissue to bond to the surrounding bone. Deep friction massage, which breaks down the scar tissue, allows more liberal and pain-free movement of the joint.

Many shoulder problems appearing at the high school level actually developed years before in age-group swimming, possibly from overtraining or improper stroke technique and improper weight or flexibility training. (See chapter 3 for proper training techniques.) We do know that in most cases swimmer's shoulder develops when the arm is elevated and the soft tissue is pushed between the upper arm bone and bone arch of the shoulder blade (acromion). A constant repeated movement and rotation of the upper arm causes an irritation that we know as tendinitis. You can do everything right as a coach and still have some swimmers who develop shoulder problems. This is where the treatment phase comes in.

Treatment.   An athlete who develops pain in the water should switch the stroke, yardage, or both for a couple of days. The shoulder should be iced. A convenient method is to fill 8-ounce paper cups with water, put a tongue depressor in each, and freeze them. When ice is needed, warm a cup in your hands until the rehab ice pops out. This icepop should be used in a circular motion on the shoulder for 20 minutes. Instruct the athlete to hold his or her arm away from the body by hooking a finger in a belt loop or, while sitting, keeping the elbow elevated on a pillow with the arm a short distance from the body (see Figure 5.11). This technique helps the shoulder by improving circulation. Monitor the swimmer's flexibility program closely, and before practices or meets have the swimmer warm up the injured area with several easy laps in the pool, a hydrocollator pack, or ultrasound, if feasible. The athlete may utilize over-the-counter anti-inflammatories (such as ibuprofen or aspirin).

Rehabilitation.   You and the athlete's parents should monitor the rehabilitation phase closely. This phase consists of flexibility exercises, such as the tricep stretch (see Figure 5.12) and anterior middle and posterior

Figure 5.11 Using ICE on a shoulder injury: Ice, Compression, and Elevation.

Figure 5.12 Tricep stretch.

deltoid stretch (see Figure 5.13), and posterior stretching exercises (see Figure 5.3). These positions should be held for 40 seconds; as progress continues, more repetitions can be added.

If the athlete complains of pain before getting in the water, pain after getting out of the water, or general aching or throbbing, or if there is any laxity, tingling, or numbness in the arm or fingers, an orthopedic surgeon or family physician should be consulted immediately. Although these conditions may not present an immediate problem, professional advice may allow your athlete to improve faster and prevent major problems from developing.

The following program of deep friction massage can be used not only as a treatment but as a preventive procedure for all types of tendinitis

Figure 5.13   Middle and posterior deltoid stretch.

affecting swimmers. This treatment should be used only for swimmers with no shoulder pain. The deep friction massage program takes time and patience. Many highly competitive swimmers and well-known teams have effectively used this program to eliminate tendinitis afflictions.

Treatment for Tendinitis

The following treatment for both acute and chronic tendinitis has allowed swimmers to continue their training regimens and avoid training setbacks. In the past, rest was the main treatment. Though rest is frequently an ally, in sports it can be an enemy, often resulting in muscle atrophy and loss of both aerobic and anaerobic capacity. This is often followed by psychological problems from falling behind the team or not maintaining set goals.

If an athlete complains of pain accompanying movement of a particular joint, and you suspect tendinitis, arrange an appointment with the sports medicine physician to diagnose the problem. Review the technique and biomechanics of the swimmer's training program to rule out any mechanical training defect that may have precipitated the onset of the problem. Then initiate the treatment for shoulder tendinitis.

First, a light examination of the shoulder will define the area to be treated. For example, if a swimmer feels pain when asked to raise the arm from the side, in most instances the supraspinatus is involved. Table 5.1 shows the relation of movement to the areas that may be affected. The team physician or athletic trainer will be able to determine the area involved and rule out any other disorders.

After the team physician has given approval to proceed with treatment, the area being tested is heated, using hydrocollator packs, for 15 minutes. Not only is the athlete relaxed by this process, but the tissue temperature is raised, thereby decreasing stiffness and increasing extensibility. This in

Table 5.1
Pain-Causing Motion and Corresponding Areas
Indicating Needed Treatment

Type of motion	Area involved
Passive lateral motion	Joint capsule
Resistive lateral motion	Infraspinatus
Resistive medial rotation	Subscapularis
Resistive elbow flexion	Biceps
Resistive elbow extension	Triceps
Resistive abduction	Supraspinatus

turn promotes an increased range of motion and allows the joint to move more freely. After the period of heat, the athlete is placed in a comfortable position. The person giving the treatment must also be comfortable to ensure that it is possible to continue a long and proper treatment.

The next phase is deep friction massage (see Coaches' Clinic 5.1). The area to be massaged can be identified by locating the point at which

---

COACHES' CLINIC 5.1: DEEP FRICTION MASSAGE

Following is a description of the deep friction massage technique.

- Locate the pain in the shoulder.
- The person giving the treatment should place the middle finger on top of the index finger, which allows for greater support and less fatigue.
- The finger must be rubbed across the fibers of the tendon, ligament, or muscle, never longitudinally.
- Note that the important thing is friction, not pressure.
- The athlete will experience pain, but that will diminish with further treatments.
- Position the athlete to attain maximum access to the area to be treated. (For example, in some cases the supraspinatus is brought out from under the acromion by placing the arm behind the back.)
- Placing the middle finger on top of the index finger gives added support and decreases the fatigue of the treatment giver. The thumb, or one finger at a time, can be used.

(Cont.)

COACHES' CLINIC 5.1: CONTINUED

- Initially, 8 to 12 treatments on each area of pain will be required. The first 4 treatments should last 1-1/2 to 2 minutes, one time per day. After the 4th day, treatments should be administered every other day, and each treatment should last 2-1/2 to 3 minutes.
- Each treatment should be followed by stretching exercises of 2-1/2 to 3 minutes' duration (see Table 5.2).

---

finger pressure elicits pain (see Figure 5.14). The team physician or trainer will also be able to locate the area if you are uncertain.

Supraspinatus tendinitis is the most widely seen lesion in the shoulder. It is indicated when resisted abduction, or sometimes lateral motion, causes pain. See Table 5.2 for the progression of rehabilitation for tendinitis.

Stretching exercises should include abduction, adduction, lateral rotation, and medial rotation and should be done through but not beyond the athlete's full swimming range of motion. After the stretching, the entire back and shoulder area should be lightly massaged for 5 minutes. This should be followed by 20 minutes of icepop massage over the rotator cuff to allow the joint to cool down. This inhibits swelling and allows the collagen in the tendon to set.

As the treatments proceed, the athlete will likely make statements such as "You're not pushing as hard" or "You're not in the right place." Those

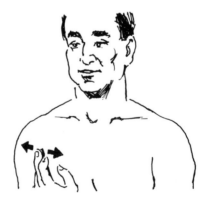

Figure 5.14 Using deep friction massage on a shoulder injury.

Table 5.2
Progression of Rehabilitation of Tendinitis

Early therapy (acute)	Post acute therapy
Rest	Heat
Ice	Massage
Compression	Flexibility
Elevation	Exercises
	Ice

words may indicate that the scar tissue is either breaking up or becoming more mobile, allowing for pain-free movement.

Through use of the foregoing technique, swimmers can continue their practice sessions and training while their shoulder problems heal (see Coaches' Clinic 5.2). In 3 weeks, begin the athlete on a weights program with low weights and high repetitions to strengthen the rotator cuff area. During the low- or noncompetitive season, use a program of high weights

---

COACHES' CLINIC 5.2: TREATING TENDINITIS

Here is an average program for treating tendinitis.

Days 1 through 8
- Heat area for 15 minutes.
- Deep friction massage for 1-1/2 to 4 minutes.
- Stretch and hold. Four stretches at 2 minutes each, light massage for 5 minutes to increase blood flow and relax the athlete.
- Ice massage for 20 minutes to cool joint down.
- Heat, stretch, and ice massage. This is helpful in the overall program, but it may be modified or self-administered to accommodate time constraints.

After day 8
- Friction massage once a week.
- Stretching before each practice.
- Ice massage after each practice.

---

and low repetitions to help increase muscle mass (see Figures 5.15 and 5.16). Throughout treatment, it is always important to prepare the athletes psychologically by explaining the program and reminding them that although there will be pain as scar tissue is treated, the pain will lessen.

Treatment time should be constructed around practice, but preferably after practice. It must not substitute for or replace practice. Continued practice is important for aerobic and anaerobic conditioning and the maintenance of correct body mechanics and strength.

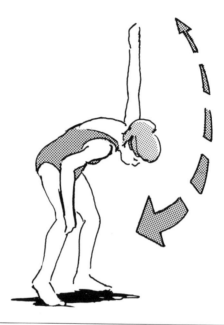

Figure 5.15   Weighted pendulum exercise for shoulder rehabilitation.

Figure 5.16   Weighted codman exercise for shoulder rehabilitation.

If movement is still impaired the 1st or even the 2nd day of treatment, the workout may still be accomplished by an aerobic pool program. This program will maintain cardiorespiratory fitness with light workouts. By the 3rd day, the athlete should be restored to full practice condition and able to do everything.

Scar tissue formations often build until they are intolerably painful for the athlete. As a preventive measure, you might have a program of deep friction massage for all team members, whether or not they have symptoms. This is no panacea, but it often assures that participation in practice or meets is not lost due to overuse syndrome in the shoulders, knees, or ankles. Unless a physician has recommended that a swimmer should stay out of practice, no practices should be missed. Incorporating the stroke along with the deep friction massage will often allow the athlete to recover quickly.

It is unrealistic to expect you to take time away from coaching to perform this treatment for all athletes, especially when your staff does not include an athletic trainer. You might try a "buddy system" where teammates work on each other, but this should be done only as a preventive measure for those who exhibit no acute symptoms or major chronic process. Cases of an acute or problematic, chronic nature should be handled only by the athletic trainer or a competent adult under the auspices of the team physician.

Breaststroker's Knee

Diagnosis.   There are three types of knee pain seen most often in swimmers. These are pain to the medial collateral ligament, which is the ligament on the inside area of the joint line (seen in breaststroker's knee); pain around the patella or kneecap itself; and pain around the entire knee joint, which in many cases may be referred from the medial side.

Pain on the inside of the knee at the joint line is coming from the medial collateral ligament and is most common in the breaststroker. By pressing on the inside of the knee, right along the ligament, you can elicit tenderness and pain. As with most of the conditions we have discussed, prevention is the best treatment.

Alter the swimmer's training program to omit the whip kick and substitute other strokes and kicks as much as possible. The constant stress of the whip kick can cause micro tears and an overuse syndrome to the medial side of the knee. Problems are often caused by the forces of the lower leg bone rotating out and the knee joint on the inside opening up. As a preventive measure, swimmers should do a 2,000-yard warm-up before swimming a hard breaststroke. If a knee injury does develop, however, have the swimmer refrain from doing the breaststroke for 2 months to totally rest the knee. Keep in mind that other strokes that are less stressful to the knee joint may be performed during this time.

Treatment.   Treatment for breaststroker's knee consists of ice, compression, elevation, warming up with a hydrocollator pack before practice, and the deep friction massage program. All of these techniques will prove to be beneficial. It is important to obtain advice from a certified athletic trainer or physician if the athlete continues to have pain outside the pool or at rest.

Rehabilitation.   Some rehabilitation techniques have already been mentioned (flexibility and strength training). The use of surgical tubing, put on the foot and wrapped around a bedpost or doorknob, will allow an athlete to turn her or his foot inward, then outward, thereby strengthening some of the musculature in the leg. Also, strengthening the quadriceps, and especially the hamstring and the lower leg muscles, will help to assure a stable joint.

Swimmer's Ankle

Evaluation.   Flexibility of the ankle joint is a valuable key in any ankle problem. Tendons that extend into the foot, and the large ligament structures in the foot and ankle, may become irritated. One technique for achieving flexibility is to have the athlete sit in a chair, place the foot on the knee, then stretch in dorsiflexion and plantarflexion, inversion, and eversion the different structures of the ankle. Each position should be held for 1 minute. These stretches should be done only while the ankle is warm.

Treatment.   The treatment for all types of ankle pain is ice, compression, and elevation. A heel lift while the athlete is not swimming has been shown helpful for Achilles tendon. The athlete should be cautioned about overuse in any type of activity while not swimming, because this will only irritate the problem more. Hydrocollator packs and mild massage, as well as the deep friction massage program previously described, have proven helpful at the later stages of the overuse injury. The doctor may request anti-inflammatory medication, but most important in treating the foot and ankle is stretching the extensor tendons.

Once again, ankle pain is no reason for the athlete to be away from practice or out of the pool. There are alternative methods to maintain cardiovascular and respiratory condition. These include using a kickboard, strengthening with surgical tubing, using a stationary bicycle, or using an upper body ergometer for workouts.

Rehabilitation.   Rehabilitation techniques include the use of surgical tubing by placing the tubing around the foot and dorsiflexing and plantarflexing the ankle. Also, inversion and eversion have been shown to be helpful. At a later stage, approximately 1 to 2 weeks from onset, exercise equipment or foot weights can help strengthen the lower leg muscles as well as the tendons and ligaments in the foot.

Other Medical Problems in Swimming

Because of the many chemicals in the water itself and the bacterial organisms that may be present, swimmers are susceptible to a multitude of infectious conditions.

Swimmer's Ear

Prevention and Evaluation.   Preventing swimmer's ear is not a major problem, provided we can keep the athletes' fingers out of their ears. Because of the irritation, the athlete tends to scratch the inside canal, causing a breakdown in the mantel on the skin's surface. This breakdown opens the door for bacterial infection that may spread to the inner canal itself.

Also, due to the constant introduction of water and chlorine to the canal, the body overcompensates and may form a wax buildup, behind which water may become trapped in the ear. One drop of alcohol can break the surface tension of the water, and it will usually drain. In some cases, however, the water remains trapped and will have to be removed by a physician. Any type of earache or throbbing in the ear should be referred to a physician for proper treatment.

Treatment.   Even though there are many good over-the-counter products that could be used, the complicated structure of the ear, and the fact that the problem might not be swimmer's ear, dictate referral to a physician.

Colds and Flu

Prevention and Evaluation.   The main way to prevent colds and flu is to keep those individuals who are afflicted isolated from the others. They should be seen by a physician and should follow directions closely. Plenty of fluids and bed rest are of the utmost importance. Monitoring temperature, nasal congestion, cough, sore throat, and so on is useful to avoid major illnesses.

Treatment.   There are many treatments for colds and flu. Ask the team physician or school nurse for ideas. Unfortunately, in most cases the cold or flu will have to run its course. In many instances an athlete will be allowed to participate as long as she or he follows precautionary instructions before and after the meet.

Nasal and Sinus Irritation

Prevention and Evaluation.   Preventing nasal and sinus irritation is often difficult. Typical problems include clogged sinuses, where the sinuses fill with mucus due to an irritation or cold; dry sinuses, where the sinuses or the nasal canal itself becomes dry from chemicals or allergies; sinus headaches due to pressure on the sinuses because of clogged sinus cavities; and runny nose or nasal infection from airborne allergens, chemicals within the pool, head colds, or viruses. The athlete is constantly getting in and out of the water and could easily catch a cold, and chemicals in the pool can cause irritation to the inside of the nose.

Treatment.   Nasal sprays might only create larger problems. Because the body tends to overcompensate, the irritation may worsen. Any nasal spray your swimmers use should not cause drowsiness and should be considered an acceptable medication by the U.S. Olympic Committee or the NCAA.

Treatments for sinus and nasal problems include hot packs placed on the sinuses, over-the-counter medication recommended by a professional, or sprays on the market that are not antihistamines or decongestants but mild saline solutions that keep the nasal passages moist. Petroleum jelly placed on the outside and slightly up in the canal of the nose at night has been shown to keep this area moist.

Athlete's Foot

Prevention and Evaluation.   It's difficult to prevent your swimmers from getting athlete's foot. Athlete's foot is a fungus that can be picked up on locker room floors or in showers in dormitories. It causes redness, itching, and swelling between the toes. There is evidence that a secondary yeast infection can develop, so any athlete's foot condition that continues for more than a week after having over-the-counter treatment should be checked by a physician. The pool surface and deck should be washed periodically with a bactericide and fungicide solution. The athlete should be given a 5-minute talk regarding shoe care and cleanliness.

Treatment.   Many good fungicides and powders that can take care of this condition are available on the market. Besides using the creams and powders sold over the counter, washing and drying the feet well (a rough towel should be used to remove dead skin) before applying the medication is important. Shoes should be left open at night so they can air out. Laces should be removed from the shoes and the tongues pulled back. It is advisable to wear a different pair of shoes on alternate days, along with a clean pair of white socks each day.

PUTTING SPORTS MEDICINE TO WORK FOR YOU

Deep friction massage should be administered at least twice a week to each member of the team. All swimmers should do stretching before every practice and meet. Hold a meeting with the entire team once each week to discuss preventive techniques, reconditioning problems, proper stretching, and what the athletes could do at home, such as proper foot care and treatment of health problems. The whole team can benefit by discussing medical problems, and they should be allowed to discuss them freely and openly among team members—unless they are of a sensitive nature, in which case you should discuss them privately with the individual.

Sports medicine is not complex, though it might seem so. The key is to focus on the aspects that are specifically relevant to your sport. If you understand and apply the techniques of prevention and rehabilitation, you will greatly increase your swimmers' abilities to meet their individual and team goals.

KEYS TO SUCCESS

- There are many people in your community who would like to get involved. Use them.

- Dealing with all athletes during the phases of prevention, treatment, and rehabilitation is very important. Know your athletes.

- Learn about all of your swimmers and have them learn about themselves. Through increased knowledge, the athlete will become more active in improving and maintaining good health.

- Use ice, compression, and elevation initially. For chronic problems, use heat (hydrocollator pack) before practice and ice massage (icepop) after practice to cool joints and musculature.

- Assign group flexibility exercises before and after each meet. Avoid overstretching, which can result in laxity.

- Stretching coupled with good flexibility can help maintain a proper balance in each individual.

- Monitor problems before they happen (swimmer's shoulder, breaststroker's knee, swimmer's ankle, etc.).

- Practice and use the friction massage method to help prevent injury or improve problems associated with overuse.

- Set aside a half hour every month to go over medical problems, such as swimmer's ear, nasal and sinus infections, athlete's foot, colds and flu, and how they can be prevented.

- Educating yourself and your swimmers is imperative. All of your swimmers should be aware of how they can help the team and themselves attain their goals through proper medical education and prevention, treatment, and rehabilitation programs.

CHAPTER 6

Nutrition:
The Winning Diet

Gale Beliveau Carey
University of New Hampshire

Mary Jane felt she had nothing to lose. She was ready to throw herself into training for the upcoming swim season. It was the beginning of her senior year in high school, and she was psyched. Sensing her drive, her coach suggested she add some dry-land workouts to her swim training—weights, running, stretching. This was her year to excel, to get recruited by a good school, maybe get a scholarship, and who knows? Maybe with the right coaching, she could be Olympics-bound.

So she really had nothing to lose. Oh, yeah, except those 10 pounds she had added over the summer. She hated being a teenager—too many changes in her body, all of them too fast!

With grim determination, Mary Jane set to work on her swimming and her weight "problem." She decided to try one of those high-protein diets she had heard about from her friends—they said it worked like a charm.

Breakfast was two hard-boiled eggs and water. Lunch was a piece of chicken, another egg, some celery, some skim milk. Dinner was fish, cheese, or cottage cheese. Sometimes when her folks got on her about eating like a bird, she'd get mad and skip dinner altogether. Or sometimes she was so hungry she'd eat everything in sight, then slip upstairs and vomit. Calories were enemies.

Within 2 weeks, Mary Jane had lost more than the 10 pounds she wanted to shed. She was training very hard both in and out of the water, but she was panicked. The weight loss wasn't helping her swim times at all. In fact, her 100-yard freestyle times were nearly 3 seconds slower than a year ago. She was doing worse than ever! Her arms and legs felt like lead. She had absolutely no energy. And the season's first meet was less than a week away.

So just before the meet, she went back to the way she used to eat, thinking that her diet must have zapped her energy. Hamburgers, chips, sodas, the usual.

Not only did the weight come right back seemingly overnight, but worse than that, the meet was a disaster! She had no kick in her legs, and her shoulders ached. She was miserable, wondering if she'd ever recover in time to catch the eye of a recruiter.

Would she?

Probably not. Not unless she changed her diet. Immediately.

Can nutrition make that much of a difference?

Yes.

As a coach, you know how to push your swimmers to maximize their power and refine their strokes. But all that hard work is for naught unless your swimmers are properly nourished. Remember, a race car is history without high-octane fuel. Just ask Mary Jane.

WHY NUTRITION IS IMPORTANT

For athletes, good nutrition is critical. Swimmers put a lot of stress on their bodies, demanding arms to reach farther and legs to kick harder.

The energy drained out must be put back, and the only way to do that is by eating properly.

To the body, food means energy. It also means structure. From infancy to adulthood, our bodies process food and turn it into one of two things: structure or energy. The body makes an eyelid or stores energy to blink that eyelid. It makes muscle, or it gathers energy to contract that muscle. Food is how we grow and survive. We really are what we eat.

Food turned into structure is easy to see—bones, muscles, hair. Good nutrition is essential for building structure. But what about food turned into energy? Food energy is fat, protein, and carbohydrate—as well as vitamins and minerals, which don't provide energy themselves but help release energy from fat and carbohydrate to the body. Food turned into energy is less visible than food turned into structure. That is, of course, unless you get too much food—potbellies are very visible.

NUTRITIONAL CONCERNS IN SWIMMING

Because swimmers know that nutrition can influence performance, they have nutritional concerns. Some of the more common ones you are likely to encounter are these:

- How much should I weigh?
- How can I keep my energy level high?
- What should I eat before, during, and after meets?
- Should I take supplements?

For answers to these and other vital questions, keep reading. The rest of this chapter will touch on these concerns plus give you some tips to be a nutritionally aware coach.

Good Nutrition for Swimmers

Good nutrition can play a major role in the success of a competitive swim team. What is good nutrition? Everyone has her or his own ideas. Some think it means eating vegetables, others think it means avoiding snacks, and still others think it means taking a vitamin pill every day.

Good nutrition means eating foods that provide the body with the necessary balance of essential nutrients, energy, and water, every day. Sounds simple enough! But putting this into practice, especially in today's world of convenience foods and fast-food eating, is a challenge.

It's critical for your swimmers to practice good nutrition, because all of your swimmers, whether they compete in distance events or sprints, are endurance athletes. They train hard, up to 2 or 3 hours a day, using the same muscles day after day, sometimes rhythmically and aerobically, sometimes with bursts of power. The energy drained out must be put back—and the only way to do this is through good nutrition.

The key components to good nutrition for athletes are carbohydrates, water, and variety and balance in the diet. Together these provide athletes with the energy and nutrients needed for peak performance.

Heavy on the Carbohydrates, Light on the Fats

Carbohydrates are one of three macronutrients in foods. The others are fat and protein. *Macro* simply means big; macronutrients are nutrients present in large amounts in food. It's from the macronutrients that the body gets its energy.

$$\text{Macronutrients in Food} = \text{Fat} + \text{Carbohydrate} + \text{Protein}$$
$$= \text{Energy}$$

Micronutrients, or nutrients present in tiny amounts in foods, are vitamins and minerals. Most people think these nutrients are the ones that provide energy, but this is totally false! Vitamins and minerals merely help get the energy out of the macronutrients—alone, they provide no energy at all.

The body needs all three macronutrients, because each serves a different function. Food protein provides the building blocks for body protein—muscles, hair, nails, digestive juices. Food fat can be stored as body fat to provide energy for the body at a later date, and it is the starting material for making some of the body's hormones. Food carbohydrate is stored as body carbohydrate in liver and muscles, or it can be burned for immediate energy. It is the body carbohydrates that are critical for keeping blood sugar levels normal and providing muscles with quick energy. It is this quick energy that is so important to swimmers.

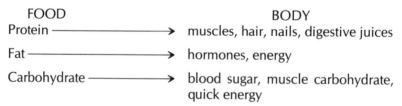

What happens when muscles run out of carbohydrates? They still work, but only at half speed. Marathon runners whose muscles run out of carbohydrates "hit the wall" and must slow down and walk. A similar thing happens to swimmers. Their arm lift becomes harder, and a kickboard warm-up takes twice the normal effort.

Carbohydrate stored in muscle is called "glycogen." To see how important glycogen is to an athlete, take a look at Figure 6.1.

The figure shows that the more carbohydrate in the diet, the more glycogen is stored in the muscle, and the longer an athlete can exercise before becoming exhausted.

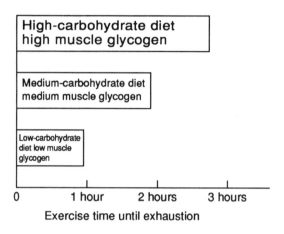

Figure 6.1   A high-carbohydrate diet means more muscle glycogen, which boosts endurance. *Note.* From "Diet, Muscle Glycogen and Physical Performance" by J. Bergstrom, L. Hermansen, E. Hultman, and B. Saltin, 1967, *Acta Physiologica Scandinavica*, **71**, pp. 144-145. Copyright 1967 by Acta Physiologica Scandinavica. Adapted by permission.

Does this mean that for optimal endurance, your swimmers should eat plenty of carbohydrates? Absolutely! And not just the night before a big meet, but all during the competitive season.

To see why, let's go back in time. Several years ago, two groups of athletes were asked to participate in an experiment. They were asked to run for 2 hours every day while eating either a normal diet or a diet that was high in carbohydrates. Muscle glycogen levels were measured before and after the run each day.

The results were amazing! Take a look at Figure 6.2 and notice that the athletes who ate the normal diet were gradually drained of muscle glycogen. In fact, by Day 3, several athletes said they couldn't run, they felt so tired. But the athletes who ate the high-carbohydrate diet replenished their muscle glycogen each day, despite their taxing workouts. They also felt great!

Your swimmers are just like these athletes, because daily and certainly two-a-day practices of aerobic laps, sprinting, and dry-land workouts will

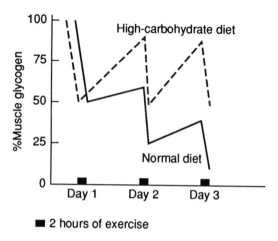

Figure 6.2   Muscle glycogen must be restored daily by eating a high-carbohydrate diet. *Note.* From "Nutrition for Endurance Sport: Carbohydrate and Fluid Balance" by D.L. Costill and J.M. Miller, 1980, *International Journal of Sports Medicine*, **1**, p. 4. Copyright 1980 by Georg Thieme Verlag. Reprinted by permission.

deplete muscle glycogen. The only way for them to replenish the glycogen is by eating carbohydrates. At the end of the chapter we'll look at some sample menus, and you'll see how easy it will be to teach your swimmers to eat a high-carbohydrate diet once they know a few basics.

How Much Protein?

It wasn't all that long ago that our thinking went like this: "Muscle is made of protein. Athletes work their muscles very hard and must be breaking down those muscles. To build their muscles back up, athletes should eat a lot of protein."

Now we know better. We understand that, yes, muscle is made of protein, but, no, it doesn't burn protein for its energy. It burns carbohydrate and fat.

Then why does an athlete need protein? First, protein forms new muscle in an athlete who is still growing. Second, in a full-size athlete it replaces the proteins that have been destroyed as part of normal aging. Third, it provides amino acids needed to make certain hormones and regulatory factors so essential for normal growth, development, and performance.

How much protein should an athlete eat? For a growing teenager or young adult, the protein he or she gets from 4 to 8 ounces of meat plus three to four glasses of milk each day is sufficient. This translates into the protein found in cereal with milk for breakfast, a 2- to 4-ounce turkey sandwich with a glass of milk at lunch, milk with an afternoon snack, and a 1/4-pound hamburger and milk at dinner. Eating more protein than this doesn't cause the body to make more muscle: *The only way an athlete adds muscle to the body is through hard, physical work and good, balanced nutrition.*

Variety and Balance

No one can survive by eating only one kind of food. If they could, they would be eating the "perfect food"—a food that not only contains all the essential nutrients, but contains them in the proper balance for the body's needs. Too bad no such food exists!

So the next-best thing is to combine many foods into a "perfect meal," letting the foods complement each other nutritionally. What one food lacks will be contributed by another. But when there are over 50 nutrients required by the body (and others still being discovered!), how do we know that we are getting what we need?

The best way to get the proper balance of essential nutrients is by offering the body a wide variety of foods, and letting it pick and choose the nutrients it needs.

Variety means choosing different foods from each of the six food groups, as often as possible. What are the six food groups? They are meat and meat alternatives, milk, fruit, vegetable, grain, and fat. Getting variety within the vegetable group, for example, doesn't mean eating cream-style corn one day, canned corn the next, and corn on the cob the next. It means eating corn one day, broccoli the next, and carrots the next. Each of these vegetables has a different nutritional strength. Carrots are high in vitamin A, corn is high in carbohydrates, and broccoli is high in vitamin C.

Remember that carbohydrates are the key to maintaining energy levels. Of the six food groups, three provide carbohydrates. These are the fruit, vegetable, and grain groups. These three groups are especially important to athletes.

In today's busy world, it is easy to get into "food ruts"—eating the same foods day after day. Many people do this at breakfast, eating cereal, milk, OJ, and toast every day. By simply varying the kind of cereal, the kind of toast, and the topping for the toast, and eating differently on weekends, the rut can be escaped. Plus, this introduces variety. Although getting variety into the diet can be challenging for young people on the go, simply making them aware of its importance may help them change their habits.

What about balance in the diet? A balanced diet means an athlete is eating daily from each of the six food groups—meat and meat alternatives, milk, fruit, vegetable, grain, and fat. Let's take a closer look at these groups (see Coaches' Clinic 6.1).

COACHES' CLINIC 6.1: THE SIX FOOD GROUPS

Meat and meat alternatives
1 ounce lean beef, chicken, turkey

1 to 2 ounces fish

1/2 cup beans

10 medium shrimp

1 large egg

High-fat meats
1 ounce bologna, salami, liverwurst

2 strips bacon

1 ounce sausage

1 tablespoon peanut butter

Milk
1 cup skim or 2% milk

1 ounce mozzarella, Parmesan, or ricotta cheese

1 cup low-fat yogurt

1/4 cup low-fat cottage cheese

High-fat milks
1 ounce American, cheddar, or Swiss cheese

1 cup ice cream or ice milk

1 cup hot chocolate

Fruit
1 apple, banana, grapefruit, orange, pear

3 tablespoons raisins

1/2 cantaloupe

40 grapes

1-1/2 cups strawberries

1/2 to 1 cup fruit juices

Jams and jellies

Vegetable

1 carrot, green pepper, tomato, cucumber

1 cup string beans, zucchini, mushrooms

1 cup cauliflower, cabbage, rhubarb

1/2 cup broccoli, onions, squash, V-8 juice

Unlimited lettuce

Grain and others

2 pieces bread—wheat, white, rye, raisin

1 to 2 cups cereal

1 hamburger bun

1 cup oatmeal

3 medium pancakes

1 cup rice, spaghetti, noodles

1 cup corn

1 large baked potato

6 cups popcorn

2 large pretzels

1/2 cup sherbet

20 animal crackers

14 saltines

Fat

1 teaspoon butter, margarine, mayonnaise, oil

1 tablespoon cream cheese, heavy cream, sour cream

1 teaspoon thousand island, roquefort dressing

2 teaspoons French or Italian dressing

5-10 walnuts, peanuts, cashews, almonds

2 tablespoons sunflower seeds

1/8 of an avocado

Meat and Meat Alternatives

The meat group provides good protein sources. Members of this group include animal products, such as beef, chicken, turkey, eggs, and fish, and nonanimal products, such as beans, peanut butter, and tofu. By choosing from the meat group, your athlete is getting good-quality protein to keep her or his muscles healthy.

A little bit of meat goes a long way. Americans tend to eat much more meat than they need; for your average-size athletes, about 6 ounces a day should be sufficient. Larger athletes need a bit more. Some animal meats are high in fat, so learning which meats are lean can be a healthy advantage.

Milk

Milk also provides good protein. This group includes cheeses, yogurt, ice cream, and ice milk, in addition to skim or low-fat milk. Like the meat group, some milk foods have a lot of fat, especially ice cream and whole milk. For your players who are lactose intolerant (that is, they can't digest milk products), there are two alternatives: low-lactose milk products, which can be found on supermarket shelves, or making their own low-lactose milk by adding a special enzyme that is available in pill or liquid form. Otherwise, the possibility of taking calcium supplements should be explored with a family physician.

Grain and Others

High-carbohydrate foods are the cornerstone of a healthy diet for your swimmers. The grain group includes high-carbohydrate foods such as bread, cereals (hot and cold, except granola), pasta, pancakes, waffles, and muffins. The carbohydrates in these foods are complex (starch), meaning the molecules are connected like strands of pearls. For this reason, starchy vegetables like potatoes and corn can be considered with this group. Simple carbohydrates (sugars) are the individual pearls. These molecules are not attached to each other. They are found in table sugar, maple syrup, honey, and most cookies and candies. Your swimmers should concentrate on getting plenty of complex, rather than simple, carbohydrates.

Fruit

Both types of carbohydrates are also found in fruits. Apples, oranges, bananas, and pears all contain carbohydrates as well as fiber, vitamins, and minerals. Although fruit juices are part of this group, many of them contain very little fruit and are mostly corn syrup. Advise your players to read the ingredients list on the juice container, remembering that the first item listed is present in the largest amount in the juice, the second item is present in the second largest amount, and so forth. If you want a real fruit juice, look for one with the fruit, not corn syrup, listed first or second on the ingredient list.

Vegetable

Vegetables are also good sources of carbohydrates, fiber, vitamins, and minerals. This group includes broccoli, carrots, celery, tomatoes, green beans, lettuce, and even V-8 juice. Salad bars are good spots to load up on vegetables, and raw vegetables are good snack foods.

Fat

The last group is fat. Food items in this group include nuts, seeds, salad dressing, butter, margarine, and alcohol. Fat also sneaks into the meat and milk groups as well as most prepackaged foods. People who eat a lot of cheese, salad dressing, regular cuts of meat, or convenience foods are eating a high-fat diet. Though fat is one of the three macronutrients and is essential for life, high-fat diets are thought to increase the risk of heart disease, diabetes, and even some types of cancer. Being active won't make a person immune to these diseases. As for their performance, athletes should remember that the more calories they eat as fat, the fewer they will eat as carbohydrate, and the less quick energy they will have.

What About Vegetarians?

Some of your athletes may be ovo-lactovegetarians, which means that they avoid eating food obtained by slaughtering an animal but will eat eggs, milk, and cheese; or they may be strict vegetarians, which means they eat no animal products whatsoever. All athletes should pay special attention to their diet, but vegetarian athletes particularly so. Vegetarians may suffer from insufficient amounts of calories, iron, calcium, and Vitamin B12. Because vegetarian diets tend to be low in fat but high in food volume, a feeling of fullness may occur before calorie needs are met. If athletes are not sure that their calorie needs are being met, encourage them to visit a dietician or sports nutritionist. Animal products are excellent sources of iron, calcium, and Vitamin B12, but these micronutrients are scarce in plant products. Strict vegetarians should take a Vitamin B12 supplement because this vitamin is found only in animal products. Good plant sources of iron and calcium are listed at the end of this chapter.

The notion that vegetarians must eat complementary protein sources—special combinations of plan foods at the same meal in order to consume the proper profile of amino acids—is based on experiments done on laboratory rats. Research done so far indicates this does not hold true for humans; experiments targeting athletes have yet to be performed. The bottom line? A vegetarian who eats sufficient calories and a balanced and varied diet should be consuming sufficient protein to meet amino acid needs.

The Supplement Story

Athletes today want a competitive edge, and many athletes hope that supplements will provide it. The shelves of health food stores, drugstores, even local supermarkets, overflow with vitamins, minerals, amino acids, lecithin, bee pollen, and sterols. Muscle magazines have advertisements that promise greater strength to readers who buy their special supplements.

Over 40% of high school and college athletes believe these ads and take supplements regularly, thinking supplements will improve their health and performance. What are supplements, and do they really help? Supplements can range from a single nutrient to a whole army of nutrients. Although they are chemically manufactured, these nutrients are identical to those found naturally in food. How much do we need of these nutrients? Wouldn't it be good insurance to take a daily supplement?

Not necessarily. For one thing, nutritionists aren't certain how much of some of these nutrients the body needs. For another, scientists say there may be nutrients the body needs that haven't been discovered yet. Keep in mind that Mother Nature gives us our nutrients in food. She designed the food and the body, intending the food to meet the body's needs. So getting nutrients from food is the best way to insure that the body is getting what and how much it needs.

One coach recently asked, "But aren't supplements good insurance on days when you don't eat right?" Sure, taking a multivitamin-mineral pill will do no harm. For some, it may be a psychological boost. But taking megadoses of one or a few nutrients can be harmful, as certain nutrients are toxic at high levels (vitamin A, for example). Also, large doses of nutrients can upset the body's balance of other nutrients. Either way, there is no substitute for Mother Nature, or good nutrition.

So what should you tell your athletes? Tell them that many scientific studies have tried—but failed—to show a performance boost from supplements. Tell them the bottom line: *Unless an athlete is deficient in a nutrient, adding extra nutrients to an already adequate diet does absolutely nothing beneficial.* Tell them that eating from the six food groups, using variety and moderation, is the best thing they can do for themselves.

Getting Enough Water

A truly forgotten nutrient is water. About 60% of the human body is water. It transports nutrients, oxygen, and carbon dioxide to and from the body tissues. It also lubricates joints. And most important, it maintains normal body temperature.

As the body's coolant, water has everything to do with performance. The heat your swimmers generate needs to be gotten rid of. Water is what carries the heat away. Powerful arm strokes and leg kicks will generate heat inside muscles, blood carries this heat from the muscles to the skin surface, and the heat is transferred to the pool water, or to the air, through sweat. Poof, the heat disappears. If the body keeps "poofing" its water without a fresh supply of water coming in, it becomes overheated. Just like an overheated car, an overheated body will wear down and eventually stop.

The body can sweat out a tremendous amount of water when trying to keep itself cool. A hard-working athlete can lose 8 pounds of water in 1 hour! Once dehydration occurs, the body's mechanism for cooling itself is broken. As you know, this can be life threatening.

What can be done? Drink, drink, drink. Cool water is absorbed faster than water at room temperature, so have cool water (refrigerator temperature) available for your athletes, if possible. One coach I know assigns a water bottle to each swimmer. By placing the bottles at the ends of their lanes, the swimmers can drink during their workouts without getting out of the pool. But don't allow bottle swapping—it's too easy for germs to spread. A mononucleosis virus nearly wiped out a whole team this way! Impress upon your athletes the need not only to drink during the workout but to take in water all day long. Tell them to drink at least 8 cups of water a day. When the weather gets hot and humid, tell them to drink until they're visiting the bathroom frequently. Make sure they understand that they should never rely on thirst alone as a signal to drink water; by the time an athlete is thirsty, it is usually too late—she or he should have had water 30 minutes earlier.

What about electrolyte replacement drinks? Under normal conditions, these really aren't necessary. As long as your swimmers are eating a good, balanced diet, they will replenish lost electrolytes through their normal diet. One glass of orange juice alone will replace all the electrolytes lost in 3 quarts of sweat. But many athletes like the idea of drinking these fancy drinks, and if so, let them. At least they are drinking. The most important thing is that they are getting water.

Now that we've seen the key components to good nutrition, what should your swimmers eat?

The Daily Diet

The ideal training diet for swimmers is high in carbohydrate, low in fat, and moderate in protein. What does this mean, in terms of food groups?

What to Aim For

Table 6.1 shows how many servings the average swimmer should be eating from each of the six food groups, per day. It assumes that the

Table 6.1
Food Group Servings for Swimmers

	Meat	Milk	Fruit	Vegetable	Grain	Fat
Men	6	4	8	5	9	11
Women	4	3-4	6	4	7	7

Note. This table assumes men weigh 150 lb and women weigh 120 lb.

average male weighs 150 pounds and needs 3,200 Calories every day, and that the average female weighs 120 pounds and needs 2,400 Calories every day.

How to Achieve It

How does this translate into breakfast, lunch, and dinner? Here's a sample menu that meets these food-group needs, for an average male and female swimmer (see Table 6.2).

These athletes are eating plenty of carbohydrates, going light on the fat, and getting enough protein. And most importantly, muscle glycogen levels are being kept high, which means plenty of muscle energy for quick sprinting and hard kicking.

Special Needs of Swimmers

Up until now, good nutrition has been described in terms of food groups and getting balance and variety. But there are specific nutrients that young athletes may be missing.

Nutrition surveys tell us that many athletes are lacking in three nutrients: *folate, iron,* and *calcium.* Folate is a vitamin found in fruits and vegetables, two food groups that young, active people often skip. Many teens are iron deficient, especially athletic ones. And because soft drinks have replaced milk at mealtime, young athletes are not getting enough calcium.

Unfortunately, deficiency of these three nutrients has more impact on females' health than on males'. For example, later in life women have a tendency to develop osteoporosis, a condition in which bones lose their density. A woman's chances of this condition occurring are less if she consumes plenty of calcium as a young girl.

Once a girl begins menstruating, she has an extra iron loss each month. If enough iron isn't taken in, the girl can become anemic. One of the telltale signs of anemia is shortness of breath and fatigue, which surely will affect her performance in the pool.

Table 6.2
Food Servings and Meals for Men and Women

How food group servings translate into meals for men

Meal	Meat	Milk	Fruit	Veg	Grain	Fat
Breakfast:						
1 1/2 cups of Cheerios					1	
1 cup of 2% milk		1				1
1 large banana			1			
12 oz. glass of orange juice			2			
2 pieces of toast with jam			1/2		1	
Lunch:						
3 oz. of tuna on	3					
whole wheat bread					1	
with lettuce and tomato				1/4		
1-1/2 cups coleslaw, 1 large dill pickle				2		
12 potato chips						2
1 pear			1			
1 cup 2% milk		1				1
Snack:						
2 cinnamon-raisin bagels					2	
2 cups lemonade			2			
Dinner:						
3 oz. chicken breast	3					
2 cups rice					2	
2 cups steamed broccoli and carrots				2		
with 2 tsp margarine						2
Small salad with				1		
1 1/2 Tbsp Italian dressing						2
1 cup 2% milk		1				1
3 cups strawberries			2			
Snack:						
6 fig bars					2	1
1 cup 2% milk		1				1
Totals:	6	4	8-1/2	5-1/4	9	11

(Cont.)

Table 6.2 Continued

How food group servings translate into meals for women

Meal	Meat	Milk	Fruit	Veg	Grain	Fat
Breakfast:						
1 1/2 cups of Cheerios					1	
1 cup 2% milk		1				1
1 large banana			1			
6 oz. glass orange juice			1			
2 pieces of toast with jam			1/2		1	
Lunch:						
3 oz. of tuna on	3					
whole wheat bread					1	
with lettuce and tomato				1/4		
1-1/2 cups coleslaw, 1 large dill pickle				2		
1 pear			1			
1 cup 2% milk		1				1
Snack:						
1 cinnamon-raisin bagel					1	
1 cup lemonade			1			
Dinner:						
2 oz. chicken breast	2					
1 cup rice					1	
2 cups steamed broccoli and carrots				2		
Small salad with				1		
1 Tbsp Italian dressing						1
1 cup 2% milk		1				1
1 1/2 cups strawberries			1			
Snack:						
6 fig bars					2	1
1 cup 2% milk		1				1
Totals:	5	4	5-1/2	5-1/4	7	6

Getting enough energy—that is, eating enough food—can be an issue with athletes, especially females. During the teens, body shapes are changing rapidly and sometimes not to the liking of the body's owner! But with time, the changes settle down. The solution is not to starve the body, though. This not only weakens the body but also robs it of essential nutrients and building blocks. It is much better to eat enough calories and burn them off during exercise, than to eat too few calories, perform poorly, and miss important nutrients.

What specific advice can you give to your swimmers to prevent them from getting deficient in these three nutrients? Tell them to

- eat from the six food groups, especially fruits and vegetables;
- drink at least 3 cups of milk each day (4 for teens);
- eat red meats, raisins, and iron-enriched breads and cereals;
- have an annual checkup with a test for anemia to see whether iron supplements are necessary; and
- get adequate calories—better to burn up extra calories exercising and perform well than to starve and perform poorly.

How Much Should Your Swimmers Weigh?

Swimmers are acutely aware of their body weights. They may not like the numbers, but they know what the numbers are. And more often than not, they wish they were lower. Americans are obsessed with weight and spend lots of dollars trying to get rid of it.

The Ideal Body Weight

What should your swimmers weigh to perform at their best? If they are too heavy, they will move more slowly through the water. If too light, their arm strokes may weaken. Only the swimmer can determine his or her best weight. Realistically, there is no magical number that each athlete must or should weigh. But there are some general body-weight guidelines for young adults, ages 18 to 25 (see Table 6.3).

Remember, these are general guidelines for your athletes. Besides sex and height, genetics plays a big role in determining an athlete's body weight. And so does the amount of muscle versus fat. For example, a 5-foot, 6-inch man at 170 pounds is overweight by the standards shown above; but if he is only 8% fat, far less than the average of 15%, then his weight is mostly muscle, not extra fat. So before advising your "overweight" players to lose weight, better advice may be to get a body-fat measurement done.

Table 6.3
Body-Weight Guidelines for Swimmers Ages 18 to 25

Height (ft-in.)	Weight (lb)	
	Men	Women
5-0		90-110
5-1		95-115
5-2	108-132	99-121
5-3	113-137	104-126
5-4	117-143	108-132
5-5	122-148	113-137
5-6	126-154	117-143
5-7	131-159	122-148
5-8	135-165	126-154
5-9	140-170	131-159
5-10	144-176	135-165
5-11	149-181	140-170
6-0	153-187	144-176
6-1	158-192	149-181
6-2	162-198	153-187
6-3	167-203	
6-4	171-209	

A local sports medicine clinic should be equipped to measure body fat. But be sure it is done by a trained exercise specialist, otherwise the measurement may be meaningless. Coaches should avoid measuring body fat on all their swimmers, just as they should avoid public weigh-ins. Public proclamation of this measurement can put undue stress on your swimmers. Being true competitors, they will compare numbers and strive to be the lowest by dieting or overexercising. Ultimately their performance and health will suffer.

Try to inquire of each of your swimmers, individually, about her or his health and weight. This will show that you are interested in them, and you'll get information from them directly, rather than second- or thirdhand. If any of your swimmers seem dissatisfied with their weights, ask why, and ask what their weight goals are. Remind the younger athletes that their bodies are still changing. And remind all your athletes that they have no control over the major determinant of their body makeup—their genes. Swimmers come in all shapes and sizes. Just look at Janet Evans standing next to Michael Gross! It's not what your size is, but how you use your size to your best advantage.

If your swimmers want to change their weights, and their weight goals seem realistic to you, you can help by advising them with the following information.

Losing or Gaining Safely

It's natural for people to want immediate results, especially when it comes to body weight. The first thing you need to do is impress upon the athlete that any weight change should be gradual, to be effective. This goes for gaining as well as losing. If the weight loss is too rapid, it is mostly water. If the weight gain is too fast, it may be mostly fat. The athlete who wants to lose weight should lose primarily fat, and the one wanting to gain should add mostly muscle. How?

For losing weight, ask your athletes to monitor how many servings they are eating from the six food groups every day, for 1 week. Giving each a special notebook for the task may provide just the incentive they need. After 1 week, have them total the number of servings from each group and divide each by seven. This will give you the average daily intake from each food group.

Next, subtract three servings of fat and two servings of grain from the average daily totals. This will remove about 400 calories. Instruct the athlete to target the "new" totals each day, encouraging them to chart their food servings daily. They should lose about 1 pound a week.

For gaining weight, the same system is followed, except now after determining the average daily food-group servings, you will add one meat, two grains, and two fats to their average daily totals. This will add 400 Calories per day; again, about 1 pound per week.

In either case, the athlete will still be eating a balanced diet. And you have provided them with good nutritional advice.

The importance of approaching your swimmers about their weight and health can't be emphasized enough. Listening to them and to other swimmers will clue you in on issues that may severely affect health and performance. One of these issues, which unfortunately has become common today, is eating disorders.

On the Lookout for Eating Disorders

Eating disorders, or intense preoccupations with food, include behavior ranging from starvation to binge eating followed by vomiting, fasting, or laxatives to get rid of the unwanted calories. Starvation is referred to as anorexia, and eating and vomiting is called bulimia. Both are prevalent in young adults today. Although 19% of college females have an eating disorder, these disorders also occur in men, and they are particularly high in athletes, male or female. Estimates are that there are 4 times as many bulimics as anorectics.

The cause of eating disorders is not known. Our society certainly emphasizes that "thin is in," especially for women. This social pressure may be too much for vulnerable personalities. People with eating disorders often are perfectionists and high achievers, see themselves as fat even when they are thin, and are intensely afraid of becoming obese.

Eating disorders can be difficult to spot, but there are some signs you should watch for. Swimmers with anorexia probably are below the minimum weight for height on the guidelines in Table 6.3. They may convey to you (or to teammates) that they are very afraid of gaining weight. You may notice that they exercise themselves to exhaustion, and perhaps that they fail to eat dinner when the bus stops after an away-from-home meet. Anorectics may also lose their hair and even show confused thinking.

Bulimia is even harder to recognize. Bulimics often appear physically healthy and are usually within a normal weight range. But emotionally they can be depressed and even suicidal. (By the time bulimics seek professional help, 5% of them have attempted suicide.) Weight changes of more than 10 pounds, caused by cycles of binges and fasts, may clue you in. A swimmer's need to skip postmeet meals, or frequent trips to the restroom after meals, could be a tipoff. Red knuckles, tooth decay, or puffiness around the face, especially eyes and below the cheeks, indicates vomiting episodes. Like anorectics, bulimics are overly concerned with their body weight and shape.

Aside from the fact that an eating disorder may impair an athlete's performance by reducing his or her energy level, it can also cause some serious medical problems. These include dizziness, electrolyte imbalance, kidney failure, liver damage, and even heart failure. An eating disorder, clearly, can be a life-threatening disease.

The American Anorexia/Bulimia Association has an up-to-date listing of centers that offer therapy for eating disorders. If you want more information or the location of a center near you, contact them at 133 Cedar Lane, Teaneck, NJ 07666, (201) 836-1800.

Avoiding Off-Season Weight Gain

A lot of athletes easily maintain weight during the competitive season but find the pounds beginning to sneak back on once the season ends. By the time the next season rolls around, they have quite an extra load to lug. The reason for this is simple: After the season, their eating continues, but their training does not. More calories are going in than are being burned.

When you talk to your athletes about their weight and health, you can find out whether off-season weight gain is an issue with them. Female athletes are particularly prone to this problem. They needn't get down on themselves about it—we all get accustomed to eating a certain amount of food, and the shift from an active to a sedentary lifestyle won't change those habits overnight.

Offer the following tips for avoiding off-season weight gain to your swimmers as your season closes down:

- It's normal to continue eating as much food after the season as during it. After all, you're used to it.
- Instead of changing your eating habits (which is hard to do), find an alternative exercise to help burn off the calories—jogging, biking, tennis. An aerobic exercise is best, but anything will do! Plus, it will help keep you in shape.
- If you don't continue exercising, remember you now have a lot more free time on your hands. When people get bored, they eat! So keep yourself busy.
- Eat slowly. This way you'll be more aware of when you are full. And when you get full, stop.
- Cut down on portion sizes, but don't cut out foods. There's no need to deprive yourself of fun foods!

Eating on the Day of a Meet

You've prepared your team, physically and mentally. You've practiced the fundamentals over and over—quick starts, proper strokes, clean turns. You've talked to them about positive mental attitude. You've educated them about their best training diet. You've come this far—you certainly don't want to lose all that hard work.

Before—What to Eat, When to Eat It

You could lose all your hard work if your swimmers don't eat right on the day of the meet. Let's take a look at some of the dos and don'ts for meet-day eating (see Coaches' Clinic 6.2).

If a swimmer eats a big meal too close to race time, blood that should be supplying muscles with oxygen and nutrients will be busy absorbing nutrients from the intestine. Consequently, the muscles suffer. Also, eating too many simple carbohydrates will stimulate the fast release of insulin from the body. Insulin is the key that unlocks cell doors and allows the simple carbohydrates to get in. That sounds good—after all, we said that muscle cells like to burn carbohydrates. The problem is that with a fast release of insulin, sugar rushes into cells, leaving little behind in the bloodstream. Low blood sugar causes light-headedness, weakness, and a slightly foggy mind—not good qualities for a swimmer on the starting block!

COACHES' CLINIC 6.2: DOS AND DON'TS FOR MEET-DAY EATING

The dos

- Eat your last meal at least 3 to 4 hours before race time.
- Good prerace meals include

  sandwiches (easy on the filling!),
  pancakes,
  fruit, or
  pasta.
- Eat something familiar—this is not the time to experiment!
- Drink plenty of water, especially if it's hot and humid.

The don'ts

- At the prerace meal, avoid heavy foods such as meats, gravies, sauces, and cheese.
- Avoid soft drinks the hour before race time.
- Don't swim hungry—hunger pains are distracting!
- Don't eat candy bars, cookies, or sugary foods within 1 hour before race time. If hunger strikes, eat fruit, crackers, or pretzels.

Remember, too, that fats and proteins slow down digestion, so it's best to keep these to a minimum. This goes for premeet as well as between-race eating. The last section of this chapter has some suggested premeet meals.

During the Meet

The dos and don'ts for premeet eating also apply to between-race eating. Snack-type foods will prevent hunger if the wait is not too long, say less than 2 hours. However, if there will be a wait of 3 hours or more, then a high-carbohydrate meal may be in order.

One thing that is essential to do between races is to drink fluids, preferably water. Have your players avoid soft drinks or sugary fruit juices unless it is very close to race time (within 15 minutes). Otherwise the insulin response will kick in, and the blood sugar level will drop.

After the Meet

After competition, your players should eat exactly what they have been eating during training—a high-carbohydrate meal to replenish those glycogen stores. Fast-food chains are the usual spot to stop after a meet, and unfortunately fast foods are high in fat and protein and low in carbohydrate. There are some exceptions, though, and there is a guide to healthy fast-food eating near the end of this chapter. Besides stopping at fast-food chains, suggest a stop at a breakfast or pizza chain. Pancakes, French toast, waffles, and thick crust pizza all make fine high-carbohydrate meals.

PUTTING NUTRITION TO WORK FOR YOU

A major challenge for you, as a coach, is putting words into action. Diagramming a clean flip-turn is one thing, but your swimmers must get into the pool and move through it, again and again, before it sticks. The same goes for nutritional knowledge. You could tell your athletes to read this chapter. Better, though, is to show them. This section is designed to help you do just that.

Passing It On

You'll need to pass along some basic nutrition information to your athletes to lay the groundwork for healthy eating. The easiest way to do this is to talk to them with some visual aids. The following are outlines for two short talks, 15 to 20 minutes each, that you can give before practice.

TALK 1

Your Goals
1. To explain where food energy comes from and how the body uses it
2. To emphasize the importance of muscle glycogen to your athletes

You'll Need
1. A blackboard and chalk

Your Approach
1. Explain to your team that, although you're not a nutrition expert, you do know that nutrition is important. All hard work goes down the drain if proper foods aren't eaten.
2. Ask your swimmers why they need food (answer: for energy). Ask them where the energy comes from (answer: fats, carbohydrates, proteins; *not* vitamins and minerals).

3. Outline the food sources of fat, carbohydrate, and protein. Explain that the body converts them into stores of fat, carbohydrate, and protein (see Figure 6.3). Explain that too much of any nutrient is converted into fat.
4. Explain that during exercise the body uses fat and glycogen for energy, but that glycogen is the key. The harder the exercise, the more glycogen gets used up. This glycogen must be replaced by food carbohydrates. If it isn't, fatigue sets in. Draw the glycogen graph on the blackboard (see Figure 6.4).

Your blackboard should look like this:

Then like this:

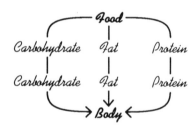

And lastly like this:

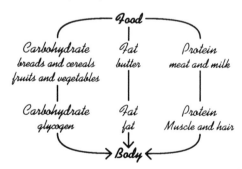

Figure 6.3 The way your blackboard will look for Talk 1.

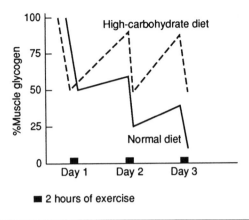

Figure 6.4   Glycogen graph for Talk 1.

TALK 2

Your Goals
1. To reinforce major points from Talk #1
2. To list foods that are high in carbohydrates
3. To explain balanced eating from the six food groups

You'll Need
1. A blackboard and chalk
2. A can of V-8 juice, a bottle of salad dressing, a carton of yogurt, a jar of peanut butter, a bagel, a portion of cream cheese, a donut

Your Approach
1. Review Talk #1 by asking your players where food energy comes from (answer: fats, carbohydrates, and proteins). Ask what happens to it in the body (answer: fat is stored as fat or burned for energy; carbohydrate is stored as glycogen or burned for energy; protein builds muscle, hair, etc.; each of them can be stored as fat if too much of it is eaten). Ask why athletes need plenty of carbohydrates (answer: to keep muscle glycogen stores filled—glycogen is essential for high energy).
2. Ask which foods have carbohydrates (answer: breads, cereals, bagels, pasta, rice, fruits, potatoes, corn).
3. Ask about the rest of the diet. Introduce the idea of the six food groups and write them on the board.
4. On your blackboard, write that a 150-pound man needs at least nine servings of grains per day, and that a 120-pound woman needs at least seven servings per day (see Figure 6.5).

Your blackboard should look like this:

	Meat	Milk	Fruit	Vegetable	Grains and other	Fat
Men	6	4		5-10	9	7-14
Women	4	3-4		5-10	7	5-10

Figure 6.5   The way your blackboard will look for Talk 2.

5. Fill in the other food groups—your swimmers should get at least five fruits and vegetables, three to four milk servings, and 4 to 6 ounces of meat per day.
6. Remind them that foods like donuts and candy bars have a lot of fat. This is OK, but suggest that sometimes they reach for a bagel, a piece of fruit, or some toast and jelly instead (these are carbohydrates).
7. Ask your players to guess which category the foods that you've brought with you fall into:
   V-8 juice (vegetable); salad dressing (fat); yogurt (milk and fat); peanut butter (meat and fat); bagel (carbohydrate); bagel with cream cheese (carbohydrate and fat); donut (carbohydrate and fat).
8. Tell them you can provide them with a nutrition checklist (see the following section), and discuss guidelines for changing their body weight (see the previous section).
9. Send them off with a strong reminder to eat their carbohydrates.

The Swimmer's Nutrition Checklist

Some of your swimmers may be more interested than others in their nutrition. This is normal. For the interested ones, you can make copies of the checklist below and of the six food groups on pages 130-131. The checklist contains questions to be answered each day until they become second nature:

_____ Have I had at least seven (women) or nine (men) grains today?

_____ Have I had three or four milks today?

_____ Have I had at least five fruits and vegetables today?

_____ Have I had at least 4 to 6 ounces of meat today?

_____ Have I had at least 8 cups of water today?

Sample Menus

Translating food group servings into healthy meals can be done easily (see Coaches' Clinic 6.3).

The Travel Cooler

A good one-time investment for your team is a cooler. You can take it on the road, use it at home to keep water and juices chilled (remember, cold

---

COACHES' CLINIC 6.3: SAMPLE MENUS FOR 1 WEEK

Monday

Breakfast	Lunch	Dinner	Snack
Cereal, banana	Spaghetti and meatballs	Meatloaf	2% milk
2% milk	French bread	Carrots and peas	Popcorn (unbuttered)
Toast and jam	Green beans	Potato and yogurt	Lemonade
Orange juice	Fruit cocktail	Salad	
	2% milk	2% milk	
		Apple pie	

Tuesday

Breakfast	Lunch	Dinner	Snack
Oatmeal with raisins	Chili	Chicken breast	Cinnamon bagel
Toast and jam	Rolls	Rice	2% milk
Orange juice	Corn	Steamed broccoli	
2% milk	Apple Crisp	Whole wheat bread	
	2% milk	Strawberries	
		2% milk	

Wednesday

Breakfast	Lunch	Dinner	Snack
Cereal, banana	Hamburger and roll	Pasta with vegetables and Parmesan cheese	Chocolate cake
2% milk	French fries		2% milk
Toast and jam	Carrot-raisin salad	Whole wheat rolls	
Orange juice	V-8 juice	2% milk	
	2% milk	Fruit bowl	

(Cont.)

COACHES' CLINIC 6.3: CONTINUED

Thursday—afternoon meet

Breakfast	Lunch	Dinner	Snack
Cream-of-wheat	Tuna sandwich	2 hamburgers	Chocolate chip cookies
Toast and jam	Tomato soup	Salad	2% milk
Strawberries	Crackers	Vanilla shake	Popcorn, lemonade
Orange juice	Coleslaw		
	2% milk		
	Fruit gelatin		

Friday

Breakfast	Lunch	Dinner	Snack
Blueberries, waffles, and syrup	Mexican salad	Shrimp and pasta	Melon and pineapple chunks
	Corn bread	Salad	Lemonade
	Peaches	Whole wheat rolls	
2% milk	2% milk	2% milk	
Orange juice	Sherbet	Strawberry pie	

Saturday—all day meet

Breakfast	Snacks between races	Dinner
Pancakes and syrup	Peanut butter on crackers	Pasta salad bar
Orange juice	Oyster or graham crackers	Rolls
Muffins	Apples, oranges, bananas	Hamburger
	Rolls, bagels	Vanilla shake

Sunday

Brunch	Dinner	Snack
Scrambled eggs, ham	V-8 juice	Popcorn
4 pieces toast with jam	Roast beef	
Fruit cup	Potato	
Orange and tomato juice	Salad	
2% milk	Peas and onions	
	Rolls	
	Angel food cake	
	2% milk	

water is absorbed faster than water at room temperature), and keep snack items in it. These are some good cooler items, especially for away meets:

- Fresh fruit
- Fruit juices in individual boxes
- A jar of peanut butter and a knife
- 3 boxes of wheat crackers
- 3 bags of pretzels
- A box of graham crackers
- Bagels

Eating on Meet Day

Premeet meals, whatever time of day they are eaten, should be satisfying but light. Here are two sample breakfast meals:

- Cereal, 2% milk, whole wheat toast with jam, orange juice
- Pancakes with syrup, 2% milk, orange juice

Here are two sample lunch or supper menus:

- A turkey sandwich, crackers, pickles, an apple, 2% milk
- Spaghetti, bread, 2% milk, banana, fruit gelatin

During a meet, your swimmers should drink plenty of water. Between races, they should snack on crackers, apples, oranges, bananas, rolls, and bagels. Also, make sure they avoid the Nos in Table 6.4.

Table 6.4
Eating Between Races

Yes	No
Peanut butter crackers	Soft drinks
Oranges, apples, bananas	Candy bars
Crackers	Sugary fruit juice
Diluted fruit juice	Deluxe hamburgers
Pretzels	French fries
Bagels	Potato chips
Water	

After the meet, your swimmers should restore their glycogen stores with a high-carbohydrate meal, such as

- spaghetti and meat sauce, or
- a thick-crust pizza, or
- pancakes with syrup.

Fast-Food Eating

Eating on the road can be tough on the budget, so most teams stop at fast-food chains. Nutritionally speaking, this can be a real challenge. The problems with fast foods are their high fat content and their lack of fruits and vegetables. But salad bars, low-fat milk, and self-styled hamburgers have helped the nutritional standing of many fast-food chains.

Below is a list of some major fast-food chains and suggestions for healthy food choices:

- McDonald's: hamburger or cheeseburger (not a Big Mac or super deluxe burger), salad, shake, sundae
- Wendy's: plain baked potato, chili, chicken breast fillet sandwich, single hamburger
- Pizza Hut: thick-crust pizza (go easy on the meat and cheese)
- Kentucky Fried Chicken: original recipe chicken breast, corn on the cob, mashed potatoes
- Taco Bell: bean burrito, tostada, combination burrito
- Long John Silver's: coleslaw, ocean scallops, shrimp with batter, breaded oysters

Good Sources of Iron and Calcium

Iron and calcium can be problem nutrients for all your swimmers, male and female. Good sources of each nutrient, listed by food group, are shown in Coaches' Clinic 6.4.

Congratulations! You're now equipped to answer swimmers' most common nutritional questions, raised at the beginning of the chapter:

- How much should I weigh?
- How can I keep my energy level high?
- What should I eat before, during, and after meets?
- Should I take supplements?

In answering the first question, remind your swimmers that they are the only ones who can determine their best body weights, but general guidelines, like those in Table 6.3, and an accurate body-fat measurement can help them in that determination.

As for keeping energy levels high, a balanced diet that emphasizes variety, carbohydrates, and water helps assure a healthy body and optimal glycogen stores.

COACHES' CLINIC 6.4: IRON AND CALCIUM SOURCES

Iron-rich food choices

Fruit	*Vegetable*	*High carbohydrate*	*Meat*
Raisins	Broccoli	Blackstrap molasses	All, especially
Dried apricots	Spinach	Iron-enriched cereals	clams
Strawberries	Asparagus	Iron-fortified breads	liver
Dried dates	Corn		oysters
Prunes	All squash		
Blueberries	Tomato juice		
	Wheat germ		
	Chicory		
	Chard		
	Collards		
	Dandelion greens		
	Brussels sprouts		

Calcium-rich food choices

Fruit	*Vegetable*	*High carbohydrate*
Oranges	Collard greens	Self-rising cornmeal
Orange juice	Spinach	Blackstrap molasses
(calcium fortified)	Mustard greens	
Banana	Turnip greens	
Apple	Broccoli	
	Green beans	

Meat	*Milk*
Sardines	Skim, 2%, or whole milk
Canned salmon	Cheese
Almonds	Yogurt
Tofu	Tofu
Oysters	Ice cream, ice milk
Clams	Nonfat dry milk
	Soy milk (calcium fortified)

When to eat before, during, and after meets is just as important as what to eat. Table 6.4 highlights tips for eating before and during meets, and these hold for postcompetition too. The focus is on complex carbohydrates and plenty of water.

The supplement issue can be a sensitive one, especially because supplements provide many athletes with a psychological boost. Inform your athletes of the bottom line: Unless an athlete has a deficiency, nutrient supplements won't help his or her performance. Taking a multivitamin is OK if they feel it helps them, but megadosing on supplements can be a ticket to trouble.

KEYS TO SUCCESS

- Your nutrition knowledge can make a big difference to your team's performance—pass it on!
- A high-carbohydrate diet during the season means a high-energy performance.
- Muscle glycogen stores are used up by hard training, and they can be replaced only by food carbohydrates.
- Carbohydrates can be complex (starch), as in bread, pasta, rice, and beans, or simple (sugar), as in candy, carrots, yogurt, grapes, soft drinks, and milk. Your swimmers should choose more complex carbohydrates than simple ones.
- Your swimmers should eat plenty of complex carbohydrates every day, not just the night before a meet.
- Have your swimmers balance their diets by choosing from the six food groups—meat, milk, fruit, vegetable, grains, fats.
- Encourage your swimmers to eat three meals a day, plus snacks, rather than skip meals. Their energy levels will be much more constant.
- Premeet meals should be at least 3 hours before starting time.
- Your swimmers should avoid simple carbohydrates the hour before race time.
- If hunger strikes before or between races, your swimmers should eat pretzels, crackers, and fruit and drink water.
- Be sure your swimmers drink plenty of cool water during the day, especially on those hot, humid ones.

Acknowledgments: Special thanks to Brenda Skelley, men's and women's swim coach at the University of New Hampshire, Durham, New Hampshire, and to Steven Ostapower, girls' swim coach at Natick High School, Natick, Massachusetts, for information on training and racing, and personal thoughts on good nutrition for swimmers.

Index

Italicized page numbers indicate tables or coaches' clinics.

About the Editor

John Leonard has been the executive director of the American Swimming Coaches Association (ASCA) in Fort Lauderdale, Florida, since 1985. As leader of the largest professional coaches association in swimming, Leonard is responsible for the professional development of over 3500 American coaches and is involved in international coaching. He has developed both a comprehensive certification program for swimming coaches and an ongoing educational program that encompasses all levels of swimming coaches. Prior to working with the ASCA, Leonard coached for 14 years, in Syracuse, New York, and Lake Forest, Illinois, producing Olympic swimmers and numerous age-group, senior team, and individual champions. He has written four books and more than 100 articles on swimming.

About the Authors

William S. Husak graduated from State University of New York College at Cortland with a BS and earned an MS and a PhD in physical education from Texas A&M Universitry. Currently a professor and chair of the Department of Physical Education at California State University–Long Beach, he has taught courses in motor learning and psychology and coaching, as well as specific sport coaching courses. Dr. Husak has also coached sports at various levels, from youth to high school varsity sports. He is a member of the North American  Society for the Psychology of Sport and Physical Activity, the American Alliance for Health, Physical Education, Recreation and Dance, and a Leader Level instructor for the National Federation of Interscholastic Coaches Education Program and the American Coaching Effectiveness Program.

Douglas E. Young received his doctoral degree in kinesiology from the University of California–Los Angeles. He is an assistant professor in the Department of Physical Education at California State University–Long Beach, where he is involved in the instruction of students and coaches. An active researcher, Dr. Young investigates issues in human movement control and skills acquisition for basic and applied science areas. He is a member of the North American Society for the Psychology of Sport and Physical Activity and the American Alliance for Health,  Physical Education, Recreation and Dance and is a leader Level instructor for the National Federation of Interscholastic Coaches Education Program and the American Coaching Effectiveness Program.

Jodi Yambor received a BA from the University of Miami and an MS in motor learning and a PhD in sport psychology from Florida State University. She was a 16-time All-American swimmer at the University of Miami, a member of two national championship teams, and is an American record holder. Dr. Yambor, who teaches graduate and undergraduate sport psychology classes at the University of Miami, has had extensive experience coaching college-level, age-group, and All-American swimmers. As the first sport psychology consultant hired full-time by the athletic department of a major university, she works with student-athletes and professional athletes from numerous sports. In 1990, she was appointed a sport psychology consultant to The Athletics Congress, the national governing body of U.S. Track.

Rick L. Sharp received his BS in physical education from California State University–Chico, where he was an NCAA Division II All-American swimmer. He earned his MEd in physical education from the University of Nevada–Las Vegas and a PhD in human bioenergetics from Ball State University in Indiana. Dr. Sharp is an associate professor of physical education and director of the Exercise Physiology Laboratory at Iowa State University. He has coached age-group and collegiate swimming for 9 years and remains active in swimming research as the editor of the *Journal of Swimming Research*. He has authored numerous scientific journal and magazine articles on physiological aspects of competitive swimming and is a frequent speaker on swimming physiology at coaches clinics throughout the U.S. and abroad.

Bruce P. McAllister received his BS from Indiana State University and his MS from Indiana University. He is an assistant professor and head athletic trainer at North Central College in Illinois and an adjunct associate professor at Northern Illinois University. In addition, he is the medical coordinator for major aquatic events at the Indiana University Natatorium in Indianapolis, an athletic trainer for both the U.S. swimming and U.S. diving national teams, and a consultant on aquatic injury management and rehabilitation to coaches and athletes.

McAllister enjoys speaking nationally and internationally on aquatic sports medicine and has written extensively on the subject.

Gale Beliveau Carey, MS, PhD, LN, is an assistant professor in the Human Nutrition Program of animal and Nutrition Sciences at the University of New Hampshire. Her education in biochemistry and nutritional science allows her to conduct extensive research in intermediary metabolism. She has also studied the nutrition and performance of the University of New Hampshire swim and crew teams. Dr. Carey is a member of the American Institute of Nutrition, American Nutritionists Association, the American Dietetics Association, and the American

College of Sports Medicine. She opted for a career in science by default at age 13 when she realized she would never play first base for the Boston Red Sox, but her interest in sports continues: She is a veteran of five marathons (including Boston) and innumerable middle-distance running events, an avid baseball fan, and a loyal baseball score keeper for the Chicago-based STATS, Inc.